4.74

Philosophers in Perspective

There is an abundance now of books of 'readings' from the major philosophers, in which the selections are so often too brief and snippety to be of any great value to the student. There are also many collections of essays and articles about the major philosophers on the market. These too are unsatisfactory from the student's point of view in that they suffer severely from the defect of discontinuity and are unable to trace the scope and articulation of a man's work, as each contributor writes from the standpoint of his own interpretation.

There is a great need for books that are devoted to a single philosopher and that are written by a single author who is allowed the room to develop both his exposition and his examination of his subject in sufficient detail. *Philosophers in Perspective* satisfies this demand and makes available to students studies of all the major philosophers, and some of the undeservedly minor ones as well, which will afford them for the first time the opportunity of understanding the philosopher, of coming to grips with his thought, and of seeing him in his place in the development of philosophy, or of his special area of it.

Each book in the series fits into this framework, but the authors are given the freedom to adapt it to their own requirements. Main emphasis will be placed on exposition and examination of the philosopher's thought, but enough will be written about the influences on him and about his own influence on subsequent thought, to show where he stands in the perspective of his subject. Wherever relevant, particular emphasis will be placed on the philosopher's contributions to moral and political thought, which have often in the past been treated cursorily as tailpieces to his writings on metaphysics and epistemology. This aspect of the series will prove most useful to students of politics, history and sociology.

JOHN LOCKE

J. D. Mabbott

Macmillan

UCG
LOC,M

© J. D. Mabbott 1973

First published 1973 by
THE MACMILLAN PRESS LTD
London and Basingstoke
Associated companies in New York Dublin
Melbourne Johannesburg and Madras

SBN 333 03169 5

Printed in Great Britain by
THE BOWERING PRESS
Plymouth

Contents

Part Four: Political Theory

Preface

The aim of this book, suggested by the title of the series to which it belongs – 'Philosophers in Perspective' – is to look again at Locke's arguments, to consider their validity in their own context, and to ask how they stand in view of recent contributions to the study of the problems with which Locke was concerned.

In recent years Locke has been well served by scholars. The accession to the Bodleian Library of the Lovelace papers helped to reawaken interest in him. With M. Cranston as a biographer, W. von Leyden as a researcher, P. Abrams, J. W. Gough, R. Klibansky and P. Laslett as editors of particular works, his sources and development have been well covered. R. I. Aaron's *John Locke* remains an indispensable general guide to Locke's philosophy and in particular to the way in which the *Essay Concerning Human Understanding* was written.

I have therefore excluded from this study any consideration of influences on Locke, of textual matters including the development of his thought, except where this was necessary to clarify his final position on any issue. I am much indebted to all the experts mentioned above. I have made liberal use of quotations to allow Locke to speak for himself and to save readers from having to check my references in order to find whether Locke really said what I attribute to him.

The attempt to consider how Locke's views would look in the light of recent philosophical developments met with some difficulty, resulting mainly from the influence of Wittgenstein. Thirty years ago there would have been no problem. Most philosophers in Britain and America were in the direct line of English empiricism from Locke and were obviously discussing the same problems and in

7

many cases by the same methods and arguments. This would apply to Russell, Whitehead, Moore, Alexander, Price and Broad, as well as to the various schools of 'realism' in the United States. The idealist tradition deriving from Kant and Hegel had practically died out. But much of this tradition had arisen from reaction against the empirical tradition and therefore provided alternative answers to the same problems. But the development of the analytic and linguistic movements changed all this. Locke himself had argued that much philosophical debate was due to linguistic confusions. But little of his actual argument proceeds by identifying and resolving these confusions. Indeed some extremists might say that in view of recent developments Locke's work has no modern relevance at all. As speculative ontology it is meaningless; as epistemology it should be taken over by the psychologists; as moral and political theory it is an interesting commentary on the English political social and religious scene at the end of the seventeenth century; but as *argument* claiming truth or validity it has no status and no modern counterparts. But the extremist tide has ebbed and some of Locke's problems reappear, though in new ways. One which has received considerable attention in the new vein is that of 'ideas of sensation', to which I refer below.

On the suggestion of my editor I have paid more attention than is usual in general books on Locke to his moral and political views. This is partly to redress the balance, but also because the Lovelace papers have much more bearing on these aspects of his philosophy than on his epistemology.

I close the writing of this study (since the Preface is always the last word) with a renewed sense of Locke's shrewdness and candour. His inconsistencies are frequent and his verbosity (especially in controversy) immense. But this does nothing to deny his claim to be the founder of philosophy in English.

I am greatly indebted to Professor Gilbert Ryle for his help in reading the manuscript, clarifying its argument, and improving its presentation.

Biographical Note

John Locke was born on 29 August 1632. His father was a Justice of the Peace, and Locke was brought up in the Puritan tradition and the Parliamentary faith in the sovereignty of the people. He went to Westminster School in 1647 under its great headmaster, Richard Busby. The Royalist traditions of the school must have tempered his previous upbringing. The education there in Latin, Greek, Hebrew and Arabic he later criticised as over-linguistic.

In 1652 he became a Junior Student (or Scholar) of Christ Church, Oxford, where he read the usual course of rhetoric, logic and grammar. After his BA (1655) he went on to history, astronomy, natural philosophy, Hebrew and Arabic. The tradition of his College and especially his friendship with Pocock, the Oriental scholar, swung him further towards the Royalist cause, and he welcomed the restoration of Charles II in 1660. On taking his MA in 1658 he became a Senior Student (or Fellow) of Christ Church and later Reader in Greek (1660) and in Rhetoric (1662) and finally Censor of Moral Philosophy (1664).

He thought little of the traditional Oxford curriculum, and from 1657 onwards his intellectual development owed most to his association with Sir Robert Boyle, the great pioneer of experimental science, and with Sydenham, the leading physician in the country. For even the scientific subjects in the University curriculum – natural philosophy, astronomy, medicine – were taught as textbook subjects with no experimental or laboratory element.

Between 1660 and 1663 Locke also began to put on paper his first philosophical views: essays on the powers of the magistrate and on natural law in morals and theology. His interests did not as yet include epistemology. His ambition outside moral and political philosophy was to be a scientist himself.

In 1665 he had his first taste of political life when he went to Brandenburg as Secretary to Sir Walter Vane's mission. The mission failed but Locke was much impressed by the religious peace and tolerance of the Dutch in contrast with the English scene.

Back in Oxford in 1666 he had to decide on his future. A Studentship at Christ Church was normally a life appointment, vacated only on marriage. Certain intellectual flirtations with the young ladies of Black Hall in Oxford in 1659 did not shake Locke's lifelong bachelor status. Students normally took orders in the Church of England; but Locke like Boyle decided against this course and proposed instead to qualify in medicine. The King urged the Dean of Christ Church to permit Locke to remain a Student on these terms. He became a very well-informed physician and worked with Sydenham on simples (or herbal medicines).

In 1667 the whole course of his life was changed by his appointment as personal physician to Anthony Ashley Cooper, Baron Ashley. Created Lord Shaftesbury by Charles II in 1666, he soon promoted Locke to be his confidential secretary and political adviser. Shaftesbury championed religious toleration against the Clarendon Code of compulsory conformity. In this he had the support of the king, whose official religion was Church of England, but who was in secret 'a good atheist and a bad Papist'. Shaftesbury defended toleration (with the Dutch example in mind) on the grounds that it made for good trade, while intolerance led to internal dissension and the emigration of valuable citizens. Locke moved from Oxford to Exeter House, Shaftesbury's London mansion, where his patron provided him with a library and a laboratory. Shaftesbury shared Locke's interest in science and was a Fellow and Councillor of the Royal Society. Under his influence Locke wrote, during 1667, several drafts of a paper on toleration. In 1668 Locke himself became a Fellow of the Royal Society.

In 1671 there occurred the famous discussion which set Locke on the task of examining the extent and limitations of human knowledge and during that year he wrote two drafts of the *Essay Concerning Human Understanding*.

In 1672 Shaftesbury was made President of the Council for Trade and Plantations and then Lord High Chancellor. Locke was appointed his Secretary for (Ecclesiastical) Presentations and then Secretary of the Council for Trade and Plantations, an office he held until 1675, when illness drove him to France.

There he made direct contact with the continental tradition in philosophy in meetings and discussions of Gassendi's criticism of Descartes with Bernier, Gassendi's leading disciple.

In 1679 he returned to England. Meantime his patron, Shaftesbury, had twice been in and out of favour at court. Though acquitted at his trial in 1681, he aroused very justifiable suspicions of his loyalty. He had changed sides twice in the Civil War and was now again plotting treachery. He fled to Holland in 1683, and Locke soon followed him into exile.

In 1681 Locke completed his *Two Treatises of Civil Government*, but did not publish them. In 1684 Charles ii forced Dr Fell, the Dean of Christ Church, to deprive Locke of his Studentship.

Locke assumed in Holland the name of 'Dr van Linden'. There he made friends with Limborch to whom and to the sect of Remonstrants he owed much of his thought on religion and theology. In 1685 he wrote a third draft of his great *Essay Concerning Human Understanding* and by the next year it was completed.

It is a sign of the dangerous times in which Locke lived that his first publication, at the age of 54, was a note in a French periodical of 1686 on how to arrange entries in a Commonplace Book. This was followed by a French summary of the *Essay* published anonymously in 1688.

In that year William of Orange, who had been advised by Locke, was installed on the English throne, and the Revolution enabled Locke to return to England and give the world the fruits of his thinking spread over thirty years and up to then concealed in notebooks, manuscript drafts, and correspondence.

In the next six years all his major works were published. From 1689 onwards he lived quietly, suffering from frequent illness. The *Essay Concerning Human Understanding*, published in 1691, was meant to be read not by theologians and clerics nor by academic philosophers (such a breed did not then exist) but by ordinary educated men. It had an immediate success and aroused great interest, not only in England but also on the Continent, where it elicited a commentary by the most brilliant European philosopher, Leibniz.

From 1691 Locke was cared for by the Mashams at their house at Oates in Essex, and was there free to write, in addition to his published works, letters in defence of them to his critics. Leisure induced length. (The *Third Letter for Toleration* runs to 175 folio pages and the letters to Stillingfleet to 232 folio pages. His last major work, *The Reasonableness of Christianity* (1695), is not itself notable for succinctness, but the second *Vindication* of it, against Mr Edwards, is over double its length.)

Locke died on 28 October 1704 aged 72 years.

Part One

Our Knowledge of Things and People

1 Simple and Complex Ideas

Locke begins his enquiry into human understanding by apologising for the frequent use throughout the *Essay* of the word 'idea' . . . 'that term which, I think, serves best to stand for whatsoever is the object of the understanding when a man thinks'. He adds 'I presume it will easily be granted me that there are such ideas in men's minds; every one is conscious of them in himself, and men's words and actions will satisfy him that they are in others. Our first enquiry then shall be how they come into the mind'.[1]

It is true that such a request as Locke's may indeed be easily granted. Much of our ordinary language chimes with it. 'What are your ideas about Greece?' 'Tell me what is in your mind.' 'Try to clear up your ideas a bit.' What is implied seems to be this: whatever conscious activity we are engaged upon (reasoning, listening, wondering, questioning, commanding, inferring) we must necessarily be 'having ideas'.

Locke sometimes thinks of these ideas as the 'meanings' of words (concepts) and sometimes as 'mental images' or 'pictures in the mind's eye'. It is assumed that, in relation to anything in the world, there can be my idea of it and your idea of it and the thing itself. The ideas are privately owned and directly apprehended only by the person whose ideas they are. This in turn leads to representative or correspondence theories of truth. I propose to examine the problems raised by this way of talking at a later stage in this work, and in the meantime to allow Locke his request, and proceed to examine the use he makes of it. We all have ideas, then, such ideas 'as are those expressed by the words whiteness, hardness, sweetness, thinking, motion, man, elephant, army, drunkenness and others'.[2] To which one might add 'centaur, trinity, fairy, ninety seven, Atlantis, Utopia'. And the first question is how we come by them.

In order to answer this Locke has to draw a distinction between simple and complex ideas. He knows that there are some ideas which a man can frame for himself. We can imagine a bulldog with white hair and black spots. His theory about such 'creations' is that the *material* for all of them comes from experience. The material is the simple ideas out of which the complex creation is composed. The mind cannot create a simple idea. Locke compares very appropriately the notion of artistic creation. The artist *creates*, strictly speaking, nothing. He arranges into new patterns his materials, paint, or wood or stone. He cannot *create* paint or wood or stone.[3] In the reception of simple ideas the mind is passive. In the image of the bulldog the colours are colours we must have seen with our eyes on a previous occasion, and similarly with all the wealth and variety of the world of a Shakespeare or a Rembrandt. If this seems inconceivable, Locke reminds us of the endless permutations we achieve in language with only twenty-four letters[4] (or, one might add, in chess with only thirty-two pieces).

How do we differentiate simple from complex ideas? Locke's answer is 'by analysis carried to its limits'. In our idea of an orange we can distinguish the colour, the shape, the smell, the taste, the texture. With some of these ideas, the goal seems to be attained. The colour and smell and taste do not seem to be further analysable. If anyone says that the colour 'orange' is further analysable because it is a mixture of red and yellow, he is confusing the colour we see with the paints we may use to produce it. Orange does not 'look to be' a mixture of red and yellow, any more than white or black 'looks to be' a mixture of all the colours. Similarly with the smell and the taste. But difficulties at once arise with shape. Locke includes figure and space or extension among simple ideas.[5] By 'extension' he sometimes seems to mean what we should call 'size' or sometimes the occupancy of a volume of space. But he recognises that 'size' is a relative idea and therefore cannot be called simple. (For example the diameter of a halfpenny is an inch, that is one thirty-sixth part of the length of the standard yard.) And as Locke, like Newton, distinguished space from its occupants, this occupancy too is a relative notion, and not simple. Space itself is said to be a simple idea.[6] But when we consider space in the absence of occupants we regard it as infinite; and

16

V exÞansion.

infinite space cannot be a simple idea *given in experience*. Moreover Locke sees that space is not an *entirely* simple idea. With time 'though they are justly reckoned amongst our simple ideas yet none of the distinct ideas we have of either is without all manner of composition'.[7] Space consists of parts (areas or volumes) and it is from these parts, or rather from the awareness of bodies occupying them or the distances between such bodies, that our experience of space must begin. What then are the simple ideas which make up unbounded space? Locke's first answer is: the (arbitrary) units which any society uses for measurement (feet, parasangs); 'the mind makes use of such ideas . . . as simple ones'.[8] But these units are all divisible. 'Could the mind . . . come to so small a part of extension or duration as to exclude divisibility that would be . . . the indivisible unit or idea'.[9] Locke finds a unit for space in the smallest *visible* area (a 'sensible point'), and for time in the 'duration of one idea in the mind' (a 'moment'). These are *minima sensibilia*, and Locke indeed estimates the minimum *area* which can be apprehended by sense as that subtended by thirty seconds of a circle of which the eye is the centre.[10] He does not estimate the 'duration of an idea in the mind'. (This would be the duration of what later psychologists came to describe as the 'specious present'.)

'Figure' presented further difficulties to Locke. For the shape of an object would seem to be further analysable. A triangular object is one bounded by three straight lines, the shape of the earth is oblate spheroid – that is, spherical but flattened at the poles. The simple ideas concerned then are: three, straight and line, or sphere, flattened, pole (if indeed all of these are simple). Locke accordingly has doubts about 'figure' as a simple idea, as he had about space.

> The extension of bodies being finite, every body must needs have extremities; the relation of which extremities on all sides one to another being that which we call *figure*. Figure also we may reckon among the original qualities of bodies, though the idea it produces in our minds be not altogether so simple as the other [sc. primary qualities].[11]

The way out of this difficulty for Locke would have been to distinguish visual shape from geometrical form. Visually such shapes as triangular or circular are not complex. A shape has a

B*

visual character of its own which may be reliably recognised and
faithfully copied though the percipient may remain unaware of
the geometrical properties associated with it. This may seem
implausible for triangle or circle. But children can recognise and
draw circles without knowing that all points on the circle are
equidistant from a given point. This is even more obvious with
ellipses. And a pilot flying over a lake can recognise its shape as
that on the map without considering the various 'relations between
its extremities'.

It is to be noted that similar problems arise over the apparently
simple and straightforward cases of colours, smells and tastes. A
given colour or taste or smell may seem to be unanalysable. But
what is the colour we see when we look at an orange? Not a
uniform shade, both because of the irregularities of the surface
and because of shadow on one side. Locke might reply that all the
colours we see are shades of orange and he has said that the shades
of a colour are modes of the colour itself, which is a simple idea.[12]
But then the simple idea would be an abstract general idea (as
the list whiteness, hardness, sweetness[13] suggests). But this would
involve Locke in contradictions because simple ideas are given
and cannot issue from mental activity and general ideas are the
work of the human mind (as is shown below, chapter 5, p. 46). If
we reject this answer we must still ask how many colours we see
when we look at an orange. One answer would be 'as many as we
can distinguish'. Another answer, however, is suggested if it is
recalled that there are *spatially* as many simple ideas included in
the visual datum of the orange as there are 'sensible points' or
minima visibilia. Now when two adjacent sensible points have
colours which are indistinguishable from each other are we to say
there are two simple ideas of colour or one? This problem is
discussed in chapter 5 (p. 44).

(i) Sources of Simple Ideas
All simple ideas come to the mind either by sensation or by
reflection. The former are conveyed to the mind by sense organs
when they are affected by external objects. The latter arise when
we apprehend the operation of our own minds within us. Confusion may arise because in ordinary modern usage 'reflection'
means thinking, pondering, meditating, whereas in Locke 'reflection' is equivalent to our term 'introspection'.

Locke notes that some simple ideas (e.g. colour) come from

only one sense and some from more than one (e.g. shape). But this raises the question whether the visual idea 'pointed' is the same as the tactile idea 'pointed' (the question raised by Molyneux whether a blind man, to whom sight has been given by surgery, on first seeing them could distinguish a sphere from a cube).[14] Some ideas come from reflection only (willing, doubting), some from both sensation and reflection (existence, unity, power and succession). The difficulties of some of these latter ideas will concern us in subsequent sections of this book.

(ii) Modes

A mode for Locke is a complex idea which cannot exist by itself, but would be real only if exemplified in a substance. Modes are of two kinds, simple and complex. A simple mode consists of repetitions and combinations of simple ideas of one kind. Parts of space and time are simple modes, made up as we have seen of sensible points or moments. Numbers are simple modes made up of units (the unity of any idea being itself a simple idea). A mixed mode is a complex of several simple ideas of different kinds, excluding the idea of substance (e.g. modesty, a lie). Locke's application of these distinctions to ideas of reflection caused great difficulty and confusion. He says that 'when the mind turns its view inwards on itself and contemplates its own actions thinking is the first that occurs. In it the mind observes a great variety of modifications and from these receives distinct ideas'.[15] These include sensation, memory, reverie, reasoning, judging, volition and knowledge, which 'are the modes of thinking'.[16]

But sensation and memory cannot be simple modes got by combining and repeating the simple idea of thinking. Memory, for example, might be defined as consciousness (thinking) of my own past, a complex idea, including 'personal identity' and 'past'. But in that case thinking (consciousness) would be an abstract general idea occurring identically as part of all complex ideas of reflection. (On this point, see chapter 6, pp. 51–2.) A similar usage (by which mode = kind or species) occurs where Locke speaks of slide, fall, tumble as modes of motion (which is therefore a simple idea) or shades of the same colour as modes of that colour, which is itself a simple idea.[17]

One further question concerning simple ideas remains to be answered. When Locke finds the origin of all new experience in simple ideas, does this mean that we start with simple ideas and that they alone are given, and therefore that *all* complex ideas are the work of the mind combining these original data (as we saw the idea of the black and white bulldog was)?

In several places Locke seems to maintain this view. For example 'as the mind is wholly passive in the reception of all its simple ideas, so it exerts several acts of its own whereby out of its simple ideas, as the materials and foundations of the rest, the others are framed'.[18] If Locke stuck to this view his theory would differ completely from those of his empiricist successors in recent times. For them the given element in experience is a *sense-datum* which is certainly complex (e.g. a round red area) or even a sense-field (in which particular sense-data can be distinguished). But many passages in Locke approximate to the modern view and agree that what is given in sensation is often (or indeed always in the case of sight) a complex idea. For example 'as simple ideas are observed to exist in several combinations united together, so the mind has a power to consider several of them united together as one idea; and that not only as they are united in external objects, but as itself has joined them together'.[19] It is implied that, when qualities are united in an external object, the simple ideas of these qualities will be given as united in the idea (for example) of an orange, while the mind has *also* the power of making complex ideas by its own volition (as the black and white bulldog). In dealing with mixed modes, which are complex ideas, Locke says they are 'such combinations of simple ideas as are not looked on to be characteristical marks of any real beings that have a steady existence but scattered and independent ideas put together by the mind, are thereby distinguished from the complex ideas of substances'.[20] The implication is that complex ideas of substances are not put together by the mind; and this is asserted in the chapter on our ideas of substances. 'The mind takes notice that a certain number of these simple ideas go constantly to-gether.'[21] Indeed the ideas given to sight are *necessarily* complex, because colour cannot be given without extension,[22] and unity belongs to all our ideas.[23]

If it is admitted that complex ideas can be given, then it will follow that relations can be given also. This is inconsistent with Locke's normal view that all relations are products of the mind's activities in comparing or combining particular ideas with each other.[24]

Later Developments. Locke's theory of simple and complex ideas had no lasting influence and no recent successors. Hume echoed his analysis of spatial and temporal experience into *minima sensibilia*. But later empiricists did not pursue the method of analysis as Locke did. Yet any empiricist theory of our awareness of characteristics is bound to face this issue. How far the understanding of the meanings of words depends on direct experience or ostensive definition is a problem which is bound to raise the distinction between simple and complex terms.

2 Primary and Secondary Qualities

Some of our ideas resemble the qualities of objects in the external world, others bear no such resemblance. Locke called the former ideas ideas of primary qualities. We apprehend through sight and touch such ideas as shape, size, motion; and external objects themselves have these qualities.

Other ideas such as blue, booming, sweet-smelling have no similar correlatives in objects. Nothing in the real world is blue or booming or sweet-smelling. These ideas are caused in the mind through the effect on the sense organs of the motions of the minute particles of which real objects are composed. Thus their causes are the primary qualities of the particles in question. More accurately the real correlative of the colour we see is a *power*, the power of the particles because of their specific motions to cause ideas of colour. Strictly speaking, even this 'power' is not an inherent quality of the real object considered in itself. If there were no minds the particles could not properly be said to have the power to cause ideas of colour. Just as, in a complete description of a pin as it really is, one could not normally include its powers, if bent, to catch minnows or pick locks.

Locke's language is seldom accurately adjusted to these distinctions, as he himself admits.[1] First he says *ideas* must be distinguished 'as they are ideas or perceptions in our minds and as they are modifications of matter in the bodies that cause such perceptions in us'.[2] Taken literally this would mean that some of our ideas are *merely* ideas or perceptions in our minds and that others are *also* modifications of matter. This would be the ordinary naïve view. Sometimes we see things as they are, sometimes we imagine them. But a careful reading of all Locke says leaves little doubt that

22

he thought that all ideas, whether of colours or of shapes, were 'in the mind' or dependent on being perceived, and some *resembled* real qualities (but were not identical with them) and others did not. For he goes on to say that whatever is

> the immediate object of perception ... I call idea, and the power to produce any idea in the mind I call quality of the subject wherein that power is ... A snowball having the power to produce in the ideas of white cold and *round*, the power to produce these ideas in us as they are in the snowball I call qualities; ... which ideas, if I speak of sometimes as in the things themselves I would be understood to mean those qualities in the objects which produce them in us.[3] [My italics.]

When he goes on to define secondary qualities, he says secondary qualities are 'nothing in the objects themselves but powers to produce various sensations in us by their primary qualities'.[4] Thus the only genuine qualities of objects are the primary qualities.

(i) Primary Qualities

These qualities are '*inseparable* from the body in what estate soever it be'.[5] Every physical object and every particle of which a physical object is composed always has solidity, extension, figure, and mobility. It may be colourless, odourless, soundless, tasteless, so these 'qualities' are not essential to its existence. The primary qualities are also independent of perception by minds.[6] They produce in us the ideas of extension, figure, number, motion 'by impulse, the only way we can conceive bodies to operate in'.[7] But since we have ideas of the extension, figure, etc. of bodies at a distance from us, it follows that particles must travel from the bodies to our sense-organs, there to produce the motions which, when carried to the brain, cause these ideas to occur in our minds.[8] Finally the primary qualities are resemblances of our ideas of them.[9]

This 'resemblance' requires scrutiny. Locke sometimes seems to suggest an exact resemblance. A circle or square are the same whether in idea or in existence, in the mind or in the manna.[11] But the facts of illusion, perspective, etc. are enough to shake any exact correspondence, and the most we could claim would be that objects have *some* shape, size or motion and not necessarily the shape, size or motion they appear to have. This must obviously

23

apply to the minute particles; we can know only *that* they have shapes and sizes and not *what* those shapes and sizes are. A further difficulty arises over the resemblance. It would follow that if ideas resemble objects in their primary qualities then if objects have shapes and sizes ideas must have shapes and sizes too. This would be the case with the successor to Locke's 'idea of sensation', the sense-datum. Sense-data have visual shapes and sizes (and colours). But in that case the quality whiteness (secondary) or hardness (primary) would belong to the ideas, and Locke's attempt to restrict the use of 'quality' to characteristics of bodies would be impossible. The further difficulties raised by Locke's refusal to regard ideas as having qualities will concern us in connection with substance. (See chapter 3.)

(ii) Secondary Qualities

The ideas to which Locke believed no quality in the object bore any resemblance are ideas restricted to a single sense: colour, sound, smell, taste, heat and cold. He maintained that all these ideas are produced by the operation on our sense organs of particles belonging to or emitted by bodies. He says that he does not intend to pursue in detail the physical enquiries about the microscopic constitution of bodies or the transmission of impulses from them,[11] and he apologises for having said as much on this subject as he does.[12] He says that if we could directly observe the microscopic qualities of bodies, the atomic particles with their shapes and sizes, the ideas we now have of secondary qualities such as colour would vanish.[13] This, however, is impossible, as it is not possible to see shapes without colours. But Locke adds that we should not suppose that it would be an advantage to us if we did perceive the minute motions which generate ideas of colour instead of colours themselves. For if we did, nature would present itself to us as a whirl of motions which we could discriminate only by measurement. The fact that what is really a minute difference in vibration presents itself to us as the difference between blue and purple or c and c sharp makes practical life vastly easier and shows the benevolence of our creator.[14] (This is an effective and convincing point.)

The problem about secondary qualities is the reverse of the final problem about primary qualities. How can we be convinced that they are *not* resemblances, in the face of our ordinary belief that snow is white, fire hot and civet stinking?

24

(iii) Arguments Against Secondary Qualities

The Lockean arguments which follow will be accompanied by an estimate of their force. *Flame – warmth / pain scenario*

First, then, Locke says that when we approach a flame we feel first heat and then pain. No one would suppose that pain is in the fire. It is an effect on us of the fire. So too with heat.[15] But why should not heat cause pain as the sharpness of a pin (a primary quality) causes pain too? Secondly, 'consider the red and white colours in porphyry: hinder light from striking on it and the colours vanish'. No real alteration is made in porphyry by the presence or absence of light, nor can we agree that whiteness and redness are 'really in porphyry in the light when it is plain that it has no colour in the dark'.[16] Now Locke himself has shown that positive ideas may have negative or privative causes and gives black as an example.[17] What he should have said is that porphyry is *black* in the dark. But the argument would still have weight. Can change of light change the porphyry? Well, why not? But what we should be inclined to say is that daylight *reveals* the true colours of the porphyry. The justification for this will be discussed later (see p. 27).

The third argument is that the colour and taste of an almond can be altered by pounding it. But it is obvious that pounding can alter only the texture (that is the size and shape of the constituent particles) of the almond.[18] This again proves nothing except perhaps that there is a connection between the texture and the taste or colour of the almond.

In this connection we may also note that the discoveries (and predictions of discovery) to which Locke rightly referred concerning the physical basis of the secondary qualities do not in themselves throw any doubt on the reality of colour or sound as we perceive them. It may still be the case that a surface which is violet in colour has minute parts vibrating on a certain wavelength. Inseparability does not involve identity. Colour is not a vibration, nor is it unreal because vibrations are real. 'Everywhere that Mary went the lamb was sure to go' does not prove that the lamb was either Mary or a ghost.

The fourth argument is that a red object seen through a microscope reveals a very different picture; the appearance of a continuous patch of red blood is seen as consisting of a few small red areas suspended on a colourless background.[19] This is an effective argument, though it leaves open the possibility that the 'true

25

colour' is that revealed by the microscope. Fifthly, the same bowl of water may feel hot to a cold hand and cool to a warm hand.[20] This does show that both the perceived qualities cannot belong to the object, though again it may be possible to argue for one or the other or a third determinate degree of heat as the true one.

Finally Locke points out that there is no guarantee that this colour I see and call 'blue' is the same shade or the colour you see and call 'blue', though he is strongly inclined so believe it is. He thinks many reasons could be given for this belief and its contrary would be without any practical importance.[21]

The upshot of these arguments is the view that colours, smells etc. depend for their existence on a perceiving mind. But it is to be noticed that the arguments themselves never support this particular dependence. Porphyry owes its colour to the light, the almond to the pounding. Even when the evidence points to dependence on an observer, the relevant determining condition is the body, the warm or cold hand, the eye or the palate.[22] What would be required for mind-dependence would be evidence that the colours we see depend on the state of our mind. Now there is some evidence that the shapes we see depend on expectation, but not, I think, the colours. There would be such evidence if the statements 'I saw red' or 'things looked blue' were ever literally true.

C'asjan? not save Locke

Berkeley extends subjective, fm 2° to 1° also

(iv) The Bases of the Distinction

Berkeley brought forward a great weight of evidence to show that all the arguments used by Locke to show that ideas of secondary qualities were subjective could be equally applied to primary qualities. But we have seen that it is not necessary to interpret Locke as holding that the primary qualities of objects are *exactly* similar to the ideas we have of them. All he need hold is that the object itself has *some* shape, size, mobility. But, if so, the problem remains why he thought this was so in the case of the primary qualities and why he drew the distinction as he did.

The historical answer to this seems to be in the influence on him of Boyle. Boyle, like Galileo before him, had drawn the same distinction in his book *The Origin of Forms and Qualities*. Locke had become convinced, not only of the corpuscular theory of the constitution of physical objects, but also of the physiological theories about the causation of colour-perception.[23] It has been argued recently by Mr J. Bennett[24] that this connection between

Patch up Locke using girl 1° 2° p61 ?

Locke follows Boyle + Galileo in

26

anticipating Kant's categories

Primacy of 1° qs. in that complex cause explains I m' t.o. 1° qs. alone & their effects.

the primary qualities and scientific explanation is indeed not only the source of the distinction but a justification of it. The primary qualities are those which affect the interaction of things; it is in virtue of their shape, size, solidity and motion that things block, contain, imprint and move other things. Thus a complete causal explanation of the world can be given in terms of the primary qualities (including the causation of ideas of secondary qualities). If we supposed 'secondary qualities' belonged to things, it would not be necessary to invoke them in any scientific theory concerning any causal sequence. Thus Locke can be regarded as anticipating Kant's view of certain characteristics as categories – as necessary for any scientific thinking – while rejecting Kant's view that these characteristics had therefore their source in the thinking mind.

There is another argument which Bennett thinks has some weight. (He agrees that all Locke's actual arguments for the distinction are effectively rejected by Berkeley.) This is the argument that, when views differ about a 'secondary quality', there is no way of establishing who is right. In the case of a primary quality there are two appeals, one to some other sense and the other to measurement. The argument would then be that if a man is colour-blind there is no appeal to another sense nor to measurement to correct his failing. But if a man were shape-blind and unable to distinguish, for example, a circle from an ellipse, his sense of touch could be brought in to show him the difference. If it is said that there are illusions of touch also, this is not conclusive because the illusion would have to be the same illusion (circle=ellipse) and on the same occasions. And it would be improbable that there should be such a correspondence. Or again we could measure the two objects (circle and ellipse) and show the victim that his failure to distinguish them *was* a failure. Both these points are valid. Yet, as Bennett points out, we still use language which suggests that we can distinguish truth from error in colour vision. We say that daylight reveals the *true* colours of the porphyry, and we call the man colour-*blind*. But by what criteria? We do in fact use two different and incompatible criteria. Bennett mentions them both, but does not note the inconsistency or try to resolve it.

He points out that phenol-thio-urea tastes bitter to 75 per cent of human beings and tasteless to 25 per cent. Under these circumstances one cannot say the taste *is* bitter. But if it were tasteless to only one human being in ten thousand we would say the

Bennett: No criterion for checking category of 2° q.

objective indep.t of consensus Somewhat so consensus

27

Bennett denies reality of 2° qs. as intrinsic "; they are consensual (i.e. depend on consensus) taste is bitter (as we say lemons are sour). So if human beings changed it would be proper to say in one generation that this substance is not bitter and in a later generation that it is. But the substance itself will not have altered and this seems to Bennett another good reason for denying the reality of taste qualities such as bitter. So too with colour. 'Similar in colour' means looking similar in colour to nearly everyone under normal conditions. Here is the first criterion, and it seems right to say that, if this is the criterion, it is an argument for the subjectivity of colours and tastes.

But in talking of colour-blindness Bennett says that we say a man is colour-blind because of a failure in discrimination and not because he is in a minority. A colour-blind man is not a man who sees red where I see green *and* vice versa, for this fact could never be discovered, but a man who cannot discriminate between red and green while I can. Similarly we prefer the colours seen in daylight to the black seen in the dark, not because daylight is normal but because in the night all colours are black. Even if we lived most of our lives in darkness we should still say porphyry is red and white. One phrase of Locke's suggests this view. Yellowness 'is a power in gold to produce that idea in us by this sight *when placed in a due light*'.[25] [My italics.] And it is noticeable that 'ordinary' daylight is not thought by artists a very 'good light' for seeing colours – still less is strong sunlight. An overcast sky immediately after rain would be thought a 'good light' and it is obvious why. In strong sunlight the shades of green merge. So again the test of a palate whether in a tea-taster or a connoisseur of port is discrimination. Now this criterion is not an argument for subjectivity – on the contrary.

Note: The problem of primary and secondary qualities is discussed in D. Locke, *Perception and our Knowledge of the External World*, pp. 72ff, which is criticised by C. W. K. Mundle (with a reply by D. Locke) in *Analysis* for December 1967.

But this is really a bit forced (artificial), especially when observer-circumstances are a construct relative to which 2 and 1° qs. do and do not vary.

28

3 Substance

Twice in the *Essay* when Locke introduces the problem of substance he starts from substances in the plural. 'The ideas of substances are such combinations of simple ideas as are taken to represent distinct particular things subsisting by themselves, in which the supposed or confused idea of substance, such as it is, is always the first and chief. Thus if to substance be joined the simple idea of a certain dull whitish colour with certain degrees of weight, hardness, ductility and fusibility, we have the idea of lead.'[1] Locke notices that if we describe a particular object we say that it is '*something* round, yellow, odorous etc.' and that, while round, yellow and odorous are ideas given us by sensation, the idea 'something' is additional to these. In explaining how we 'make' our ideas of substances he says:

> the mind . . . takes notice . . . that a . . . number of these simple ideas go constantly together, which being presumed to belong to one thing . . . are called, so united in one subject, by one name, . . . because . . . not imagining how these simple ideas can subsist by themselves, we accustom ourselves to suppose some substratum wherein they do subsist and from which they do result, which therefore we call substance.[2]

It would seem that Locke is saying that we do not invoke the idea of substance until we have had repeated experience of a number of simple ideas going constantly together. Stillingfleet asks whether this 'custom' is 'grounded upon true reason or not'.[3] Locke replies that, in the passages quoted, he is explaining not how we come by the general idea of substance but how we come by the ideas of

particular substances, such as man, horse, gold.[4] The account of
the general idea of substance lies in 'a supposition of he knows not
what support of such qualities which are capable of producing
simple ideas in us'.[5] The reason for the supposition is that 'we
cannot imagine how simple ideas can subsist by themselves'. It is
clear that this will apply as much to a single simple idea as to a
group of them; and, in replying to Stillingfleet, Locke clears up
this point.

> All the ideas of all the sensible qualities of a cherry come into
> my mind by sensation. . . . The ideas of these qualities . . . are
> perceived by the mind to be . . . inconsistent with existence . . .
> hence the mind perceives their necessary connection with in-
> herence, or being supported, which being a relative idea, super-
> added to *the red colour in a cherry*, the mind frames the correlative
> idea of a support.[6]

Locke in fact agrees with Stillingfleet that the idea of substance *is*
grounded on reason, that is, on the awareness of a necessary connection and not on custom.

Stillingfleet's main criticism then follows. 'If the general idea
of substance be grounded upon plain and evident reason, then we
must allow an idea of substance which comes not in by sensation
or reflection and so we may be certain of something which we have
not by these ideas'.[7] And indeed this idea does seem to be the first
breach in Locke's empiricism.

His first answer is: 'I never denied that the mind could frame to
itself ideas of relation.' But substance is not an idea of relation; the
relation in question is 'supporting' or 'inhering'. So Locke goes on
to say: 'But because a relation cannot be founded in nothing or be
the relation of nothing, and the thing here related as a supporter
or a support is not represented to the mind by any clear and
distinct idea, therefore the obscure indistinct vague idea of thing
or something is all that is left to be the positive idea . . . that
general indetermined idea of something is by the abstraction of
the mind derived also from the simple ideas of sensation and
reflection.'[8] But Locke nowhere shows how 'a general idea of
something' could be 'abstracted' from such ideas as yellow, round,
bitter. Either it must be abstractable only from some ideas or from
all. It is difficult to see how some qualities rather than others
should include this idea. If it is abstractable from all ideas, then

30

any one simple idea, say 'yellow', must include the idea of 'something'. But the complex idea 'something yellow' already includes the 'general notion of substance' and the derivation seems to be circular. Thus it seems that Locke fails to meet Stillingfleet's challenge, and the idea of substance is indeed a weakness in his empiricist theory of the origin of our ideas. Locke himself was aware of this; for, on the first occurrence of the idea of substance in the *Essay*, he says it is an idea 'which we neither have nor can have by sensation or reflection'. This passage occurs in his attack on innate ideas and he adds that if we had the idea of substance it would have to be given us by nature, but in fact we have no such clear idea at all.

> If nature took care to provide us any ideas, we might well expect they should be such as by our own faculties we cannot procure to ourselves; but we see, on the contrary, that since by those ways whereby our ideas are brought into our minds this [the idea of substance] is not, we have no such clear idea at all, but only an uncertain supposition of we know not what; i.e. of something whereof we have no particular distinct positive idea, which we take to be the substratum or support of those ideas we know.[9]

No such Thing.

These complaints about our idea of substance are frequent in Locke and need consideration. First he says the idea we have is 'uncertain'. But under pressure from Stillingfleet he agrees that it is logically necessitated by the idea of any quality. 'Sensible qualities carry the supposition of substance along with them but not intermitted by the senses with them. . . . By carrying with them a supposition I mean that sensible qualities imply a substratum to exist in'.[10] The same argument applies to minds. 'We experiment [sc. experience] in ourselves thinking. The idea of this action or mode of thinking is inconsistent with the idea of self-subsistence and therefore has a *necessary connection* with a support or subject of inhesion: the idea of that support is what we call substance'.[11] (My italics.) What can be more certain than a logical necessity?

Locke also frequently describes the substratum as *unknown*; 'a supposition of we know not what'. But suppose we did know what the substratum was; we should know only further qualities of it. As he says himself

31

If anyone should be asked what is the subject wherein colour or weight inheres he would have nothing to say but the solid extended parts; and if he were demanded what is it that solidity and extension inhere he would not be in a much better case than the Indian . . . who, saying that the world was supported by a great elephant, was asked what the elephant rested on; to which his answer was – a great tortoise. But . . . pressed to know what gave support to the broad-backed tortoise replied – something he knew not what.[12]

But obviously, as Leibniz said, 'it is no wonder that we can conceive nothing particular in this subject. It must be so indeed since we have already separated from it all the attributes in which we could conceive any detail.'[13] The difficulties arise partly because Locke does not keep in view his distinction between ideas of particular substances and the general idea of substance. He himself raises the problem when he challenges those who assert a belief in substance

to consider whether applying it, as they do, to the infinite incomprehensible God, to finite spirit, and to body it be in the same sense and whether it stands for the same idea when each of these so different beings are called substances. If so, whether it will thence follow that God, spirits, and body, agreeing in the same common nature of substance, differ not any otherwise than in a bare different modification of that substance, as a tree and a pebble being in the same sense body, and agreeing in the common nature of body differ only in a bare modification of that common matter, which will be a very harsh doctrine. If they say they apply it to God, finite, spirit, and matter, in three different significations . . . if the name substance stands for three distinct ideas they would do well to make known those distinctive ideas . . . and if they can thus make three distinct ideas of substance, what hinders why another may not make a fourth?[14]

But it is obvious, when the general idea is distinguished from ideas of particular substances, that the 'harsh doctrine' of the first alternative is the right one. God differs from finite spirits and spirits from bodies only in qualities or attributes or 'modifications' (as a tree differs from a pebble); and after his debate with Stillingfleet Locke came to see this. 'The general idea of substance being the same everywhere, the modification of thinking joined to it makes it a spirit, . . . as on the other side substance that has the modification of solidity is matter.'[15] Here, as elsewhere, Stilling-fleet's criticism compels Locke to clear up the confusion in the *Essay*.

Another confusion which besets the treatment of substance in the *Essay* is that between quality and substance on the one hand and ideas and reality on the other. This comes out in the phrase 'some substratum wherein they [simple ideas] do subsist and from which they do result',[16] or when he refers to simple ideas 'coexisting in such, though unknown, cause of their union'.[17] The same notion is expressed more fully in Draft C. of his *Essay* 'a collection of several simple ideas which are united together in a supposed but unknown cause of their subsistence and union so that by substance or the subject wherein we think they inhere we mean nothing else but the unknown cause of their union and coexistence'.[18]

Locke's agnosticism about the nature of real objects, then comes in to explain why he says the idea of substance is an idea of something 'unknown' or 'obscure' or 'secret'. Combinations of simple ideas 'exist together and are therefore supposed to flow from the particular internal constitution or unknown essence of that substance'.[19]

There are two other confusions connected with this: first, the notion that a substance means something independent of human perceptions or thought; and second, the notion that a substance means something independent not only of any relations to human minds but of any relations to anything else at all. But it is clear that Locke's whole argument excludes these limitations. For if my senses give me the ideas of round, yellow and bitter I have necessarily to frame the idea of a support *for these* ideas. Hence, my idea of an orange is a complex idea of something round, yellow and bitter.

There is a further limitation which does not affect Locke's argument, and that is the restriction of the use of substance to something lasting through time. Locke discusses this problem as the problem of identity, but nowhere takes endurance through time as a necessary characteristic of substance.

It seems clear that, if Locke starts with the belief that only qualities are given to sensation or introspection, he will inevitably be driven to admit that the idea of substance is logically necessi-

33

tated by them, and therefore is inexplicable on his empiricist theory, which was Stillingfleet's claim.

There are only two ways out of this difficulty. One is that taken by Berkeley and Hume: to maintain that nothing but qualities are given, and that the idea of substance is not necessitated by them. A thing just *is* a collection of qualities.

The alternative is stated by Leibniz and is surely the correct one. It denies that qualities alone are given to sensation or introspection. 'The knowledge of the concrete always precedes that of the abstract – the hot thing rather than heat [sc. is given].'[20] Or again: 'It is rather the concretum as wise, warm, shining which arises in our minds than the abstractions or qualities ... as knowledge, heat, light.'[21]

Later Developments. The solution of Leibniz is that adopted in recent epistemology. What is given is a sense-datum or a sensum (or a sense field in which sense-data or sensa can be distinguished). A specimen sense-datum would be a round red patch, or something cool and smooth. When I look at a candle flame I perceive not yellowness but something yellow and this something yellow has a roughly elliptical shape. It is difficult to find arguments for anything so obvious. But when I look at the flame and press one eyeball sideways I see double. But what is double? – not the yellowness or the shape, but the 'patches' which possess these qualities. When I look at the sun and then look away at a white surface I see an after-image, a round green patch. I do not see greenness and see roundness and then by inference put them together, still less do I have to wait for them to be 'customarily associated' to attribute them to the same 'thing'. They are given together, and 'together' does not mean any sort of togetherness such as simultaneity or contiguity or inclusion in the same field of view. It is that specific sort (which is not further analysable) 'belonging to the same subject'. What is given to sight, then, is not qualities but something-with-qualities and the problem of how we get from qualities given to something to which they belong is a mistaken problem altogether.

Why has this not been realised? For two reasons I think: first, because of the confusions noted above; and second, because the word 'substance' is misleading as a description of Locke's main problem. If I say 'when I see double I see two substances both yellow and elliptical' or if I call an after-image 'a round green substance', I shall certainly be taken to imply that these sub-

34

stances exist independently of my mind and are continuing realities. Thus I think 'substance' is an unsatisfactory term. The term 'particular' would be better, with the term 'continuant' for lasting objects. 'Substance' could then vanish as a technical term.

When it is stated above that 'recent epistemology' involves sense-data or sensa it must be noted that some even more recent philosophy rejects entirely the whole concept of data of direct awareness which is common to Locke and the sense-datum theorists. This will be more fully considered later (see chapter 9, pp. 75–6).

4 Power

Besides the idea of substance, the other idea which notoriously gives trouble to empiricists is that of cause. Locke discusses this under the heading of 'power'. But the use of 'power' is wider than that of 'cause'. Fire has a power to melt gold and gold has a power to be melted. 'Power' here is equivalent simply to potentiality or, as Locke calls it, 'faculty'.[1] What we call 'causality' is for Locke 'active power'. One of the longest chapters in the *Essay* (II xxi) is allocated to the idea of power but almost the whole of it concerns free will which is discussed below (chapter 6, p. 65).

Locke says we get the idea of power from observing how our ideas change and 'concluding that changes will in future be made in the same things by like agents and by the like ways; considers in one thing the possibility of having any of its simple ideas changed and in another the possibility of making that change'.[2]

But here Locke is confusing potentiality with causality. If I observe a man change colour I can say 'now he is pale but he *can* blush'. I say nothing about the causes of the change. Much of our descriptions of things and people are in terms of powers (capabilities, faculties). For instance, we call things 'seeds' or 'ball bearings'; we describe weather and women as changeable; we give people 'characters' which describe, not their observable features (redhaired, stocky), but their powers (clever, a good linguist). All of these descriptions assert not what anything is but what it is able to be or do; and there is no reference to causality throughout.

Besides this confusion, Locke falls into another difficulty. In the passage quoted he confuses (as often) ideas and things. (Compare 'considers in one thing the possibility of having any of *its*

36

simple ideas changed'.) We can speak of 'potentiality' only in connection with continuing objects. A chameleon can change colour but red and round cannot change or become white or square. What is required here then is a prior discussion about the idea of identity through time. This discussion had to await Hume.

Locke is also uncertain whether to call power a simple idea. He says it includes relation (a relation to action or change) but adds, 'as indeed which of our ideas when attentively considered does not? Our ideas of extension duration and number do they not all contain in them a secret relation of their parts? Figure and motion have something relative in them much more visibly: and sensible qualities, as colours and smells, etc., what are they but the powers of different bodies in relation to our perception etc?'[3] (Here again is the confusion between ideas and things. Our simple idea of blue is not a power in bodies.)

Locke concludes that our idea of power may have a place among our simple ideas. This is clearly inconsistent, and the argument in its favour – that all our simple ideas include relations – is mistaken. The motive for this inconsistency is his recognition that 'powers make up so great a part of our complex ideas of natural substances'[4] and are therefore among the products of any analysis of these complex ideas. This is obvious in a passage in Draft C. 'For the power of being melted but not wasted by the fire, of being dissolved in aqua regia, are simple ideas as necessary to make up our complex idea of gold as its colour or weight'.[5]

It remains to consider how Locke thinks we obtain the idea of cause (or 'active power'). He maintains that we obtain it 'both from reflection and from sensation: for observing in ourselves that we can at pleasure move several parts of our bodies which were at rest; the effects, also, that natural bodies are able to produce in one another, occurring every moment to our senses, we both these ways get the idea of power'.[6] The suggestion here is that every change we observe through our senses carries with it the notion that it is caused by some activity of another 'natural body'. (We postpone the evidence of reflection.) But Locke elsewhere sees that this assumption about the continuous evidence of causation in the physical world is mistaken for two reasons. First, because what we call causation of a movement is usually simply the transmission of it. All matter is passive.[7] Second, and much more important, the

37

mind cannot see any necessary connection between its ideas of sensation. 'The things that, as far as our observation reaches, we constantly find to proceed regularly, we may conclude do act by a law set them; but yet by a law that we know not; whereby though causes work steadily and effects constantly flow from them, yet their connexions and dependencies being not discoverable in our ideas, we can have but an experimental knowledge of them.'[8] As an example: 'When a countryman says the cold freezes water, though the word freezing seems to impart some action, yet truly it signifies nothing but this effect, that water that was before fluid has become hard and consistent without containing any idea of the action whereby it is done.'[9] Here is the regularity theory of causation. From a simple occurrence of a sequence no connection is discoverable. When a number of similar sequences occur, we may infer, with probability only, to a connection, but we never apprehend the necessity of a causal law. Here is Hume's theory.

But as usual Locke does not succeed in maintaining this Humean view steadily and consistently. The passage already quoted on the origin of our idea of power '. . . concluding that like changes will be made in the same things by like agents. . . .'[10] implies that we can observe that a change has been made in this thing by this agent. Again, in the section specifically entitled "Of Cause and Effect", he asserts that causal efficacy can be directly observed. 'In the notice that our senses take of the constant vicissitudes of things we cannot but observe that several particular both qualities and substances begin to exist, and that they receive this their existence from the due application and operation of some other being . . . thus finding that in . . . wax fluidity, which is a simple idea that was not in it before, is constantly produced by the application of a certain degree of heat we call the simple idea of heat in relation to fluidity in wax the cause of it.'[11]

Even when Locke is maintaining the regularity theory, he still differs seriously from Hume. Throughout the passage quoted above (IV iii 29) he shows complete confidence that there are causal laws though we cannot be certain what they are. Hume, introducing his famous discussion, said that there were two questions: 'First, for what reason we pronounce it *necessary* that everything whose existence has a beginning should also have a cause? Secondly, why we conclude that such particular causes must necessarily have such particular effects?'[12] He sees rightly that the question of the general principle is prior to that of particular causal laws and deals with it first, by showing it is neither self-evident nor demonstrable. He then adds:

> Since it is not from knowledge or any scientific reasoning that we derive the opinion of the necessity of a cause to every new production that opinion must necessarily arise from observation and experience. The next question, then, should naturally be *how experience gives rise to such a principle?* But as I find it will be more convenient to sink this question in the following *why we conclude that such particular causes must necessarily have such particular effects and why we form an inference from one to another?*, we shall make that the subject of our further enquiry. 'Twill, perhaps, be found in the end that the same answer will serve for both questions.[13] [Italics in original.]

Hume then proceeds to give the regularity theory as his answer to the second question, just as Locke does. But the first question is sunk without trace; and it is difficult to see how a regularity theory (based on similarities between particular events) could possibly explain the belief in the general principle.

What then has Locke to say about the general principle 'that every event that has a beginning must necessarily have a cause'? From various passages in the *Essay* he seems to regard this principle as known for certain. For example, 'whatever change is observed, the mind must collect a power somewhere able to make that change'.[14]

'Man knows by an intuitive certainty that bare nothing can no more produce any real being than it can be equal to two right angles', from which it follows that 'what had a beginning must be produced by something else'.[15] As with the discussion on substance, Stillingfleet's criticism brought out clearly Locke's view. ' "Everything that has a beginning must have a cause" is a true principle of reason or a proposition certainly true; which we come to know . . . by contemplating our ideas and perceiving that the idea of a beginning to be is necessarily connected with the idea of some operation, and the idea of operation with the idea of something operating which we call a cause.'[16] This is not inconsistent with Locke's general theory of knowledge as it is with Hume's, for, as we shall see, Locke believed that many *propositions* (of which this is one) are not derived from experience but are self-evident or demonstrable. It is ideas and not propositions which must have their source in experience (see below, chapter 9). We saw how Locke failed to provide such a source for the idea of substance. But in the case of cause he does attempt an answer. The crucial idea is that of 'operating' or 'active power'. We have noted his doubts whether active power can be observed in sensation of physical objects. He would therefore 'direct our minds to the consideration of god and spirits, for the clearest idea of active powers'.[17] 'We find in ourselves a power to begin or forbear continue or end several actions of our minds and motions of our bodies barely by a thought or preference of the mind ordering or as it were commanding the doing or not doing such and such a particular action.'[18] Here then is the solution. In the external world we observe only sequences. As the sun set the air grew cold. But, as the sun set, I reached the station, the train came in, the ticket collectors changed over. The first of these is shown to be causal by its regular repetition, unlike the others. But when I decide to think of a number or to move my arm and the number appears and my arm moves, I do not need repeated experience to *know* that my decision and these events are necessarily connected, and that the connection is causal.

With regard to motions of the body this is a doubtful view. We can see children discovering how to move their limbs by experiment. There is no observed necessary connection between willing a motion and the motion. This is confirmed by the evidence of people who have lost their powers of movement and have to relearn them.[19] We discover that we can move our arms. But many of us never discover how to move our scalps or our ears. When we learn to play golf the professional says 'That's it. You've got it. Now do it again'. And for the life of us we cannot. It might be thought that control over our own minds was more directly known than control over our own bodies. But here too all the same difficulties arise. We cannot solve puzzles at once. Some of us cannot even imagine a white dog with black spots. It was one of my childhood tragedies that I was never able to recapture the rapture of a dream about a vast marshalling yard full of superb railway engines. So, after all, Locke's argument fails and active power, like substance, remains an exception to his empiricist principles.

Later discussions of causality have tended to follow Hume and to accept the regularity theory and to 'sink the question' of the general principle of causality. When recognised, the general principle is treated as a heuristic principle, that is as an instruction to scientists how to proceed, and therefore as neither true or false.

5 Abstract General Ideas

Locke notes that words hardly ever stand for particular objects or particular ideas. If every idea which occurred had a name, names would be endless.[1] Only proper names indicate particular objects. 'The white horse threw the groom.' What kind of idea do these words (white, horse, throw, groom) indicate and how do we come by them? 'The senses . . . let in particular ideas and the mind by degrees growing familiar with some of them they are lodged in the memory and names got to them. Afterwards the mind proceeding further abstracts them and by degrees learns the use of general names.'[2]

Locke describes the process as involving two separate operations. The first he calls 'abstraction'. This is the process of separating an idea from all other ideas which 'accompany it in its real existence',[3] separating it from 'the circumstances of real existence as time place or any other concomitant ideas'.[4] Thus, perceiving a sheet, we may separate its whiteness from its shape, motion, size, situation etc. But this would still leave us with a particular shade of colour, and it would not explain how the word 'white' can be used for things other than the sheet. Locke gives two explanations: the 'Sign Theory', and an explanation which may be termed the 'Resemblance Theory'.

(i) The Sign Theory

This theory explains the wide application of the word 'white' by saying that the mind makes the whiteness of the sheet stand as a representative of other whitenesses, of snow, chalk, etc. Thus a general idea is an abstracted particular idea made to stand for all other particulars of the same sort.

42

For having received from paper, lilies, snow, chalk and several other substances the selfsame sort of ideas which perfectly agree with that which it formerly received from milk it makes use but of one idea to contemplate all existing of that kind, whereby that one idea becomes as it were a representative of all particulars that agree with it and so is a general idea. . . . By this way of considering them, ideas taken from particular things become universal . . . as standards to rank real existences into sorts as they agree with those patterns.[5]

Thus there are not two different kinds of ideas, general and particular. All ideas are particular, but some particular ideas are made to stand for others which 'agree with them'. Similarly a member of parliament is not a being completely different from other men, not a beast or an angel; he is a particular man standing as representative of a number of other particular men who (in a different sense) 'agree with him'.

This theory is the theory adopted by Berkeley and Hume, in reaction against Locke's other theory which we shall shortly be considering. For example: 'An idea which considered in itself is particular becomes general', Berkeley argues, 'by being made to represent or stand for all other particular ideas of the same sort.'[6] 'All general ideas', Hume states, 'are in reality particular ones attached to a general term which recalls upon occasion other particular ones that resemble in certain circumstances the idea present to the mind.'[7]

This theory seems to have been Locke's first unstudied attempt to deal with the problem, as Aaron suggests.[8] Passages in the *Essay* itself suggest it, but they are comparatively few and tend to be confused with Locke's other view, which was certainly his final answer, as his controversy with Stillingfleet showed. Typical references to this first theory in the *Essay* are the following: 'This is called abstraction whereby ideas taken from particular beings become general representatives of all the same kind, and their names general names, applicable to whatever exists conformable to such abstract ideas.'[9] (This passage goes on to echo the examples given in Draft C – milk, chalk, snow – thus suggesting its origin.) 'Ideas become general by separating them from the circumstances of time and place, and any other ideas that may determine them to this or that particular existence. By this way of abstraction they are made capable of representing more individuals than one, each

43

of which having in it a conformity to that abstract idea is, as we call it, of that sort.'[10]

Locke's dissatisfaction with the sign theory is very natural. What other individuals does the general idea represent? Those 'of the same sort'; those which 'agree' with it, 'conform' to it; those which 'resemble' or 'are similar' to it. But we can obviously ask: what are the *features* which determine the sort, what are the *aspects* in which these ideas agree or resemble each other; and the set of features or aspects will be the general idea. Berkeley himself admits that he can 'consider a figure merely as triangular without attending to the particular qualities of the angles or relations of the sides. In like manner we may consider Peter so far forth as man or so far forth as animal without framing the forementioned abstract idea, inasmuch as all that is perceived is not considered'.[11] Berkeley and Hume also make their task easier by taking such general ideas as man and triangle (substantive terms). With qualities, the position is not so easy. As we have seen the 'particular idea' in Locke's example is not milk but the whiteness of milk, and the other similar ideas are the whiteness of snow, chalk etc. Now it is not clear what this 'particular whiteness of milk' means. If it means a determinate shade of whiteness, then there is nothing logically impossible in two drops of milk having the same determinate shade. (This shade will have no *name*.) Now, when the two drops both have this shade, is it one quality or two? 'Same sort' 'resemble' 'similar' – all seem inappropriate. But if it is one quality, this shade would itself seem to be a general idea. We have seen above that Locke would find this difficulty even more acute, for according to him each colour (white, blue, red) is a simple idea and shades are modes of these ideas.[12] Simple ideas are *given* and then minds cannot create one. But 'white' (in milk, snow, chalk) is a general idea and, as we shall see, Locke held that general ideas are mind-made.

(*ii*) *The 'Resemblance' Theory*
Locke, then, held another and quite different view of the nature of general ideas. In describing how children come to use the word 'man', he says that they

> observe that there are a great many other things in the world that, in some common agreements of shape and several other qualities, resemble their father and mother . . . they frame an

idea which they find those many particulars do partake in; and
to that they give with others the name 'man' for example. And
thus they come to have a general name and a general idea;
wherein they make nothing new but only leave out of the
complex idea they had of Peter and James, Mary and Jane,
that which is peculiar to each and retain only what is common
to them all. . . .[13]

Observing that several things that differ from their idea of
man . . . yet have certain qualities wherein they agree with
man, by retaining only those qualities and uniting them into
one idea, they have again another and more general idea . . .
which new idea is made not by any new addition but only as
before, by leaving out the shape and some other properties
signified by the name man and retaining only a body with life,
sense, and spontaneous motion comprehended under the name
animal.[14]

Thus 'every more general term stands for such an idea and is but a
part of any of those contained under it.'[15] Abstract general ideas
are the *meanings* of general terms. 'Animal' means 'body with life,
sense and spontaneous motion' and these are the characteristics
found in all animals.

Although Locke's normal view of abstract ideas is the second
theory expounded above, which considers them to be the quality
or group of qualities common to a class of particulars, he shows
no clear awareness of the difference between this and the first,
the 'sign', theory; and the last reference to abstract ideas in any
of his writings appears to lump the two theories together. Univer-
sality consists 'only in representation abstracting from particulars.
An idea of a circle of an inch diameter will represent, where or
wheresoever existing all the circles of an inch diameter, and that
by abstracting from time and place. And it will also represent all
circles of any bigness by abstracting also from that particular
bigness and retaining only the relation of equidistance of the
circumference from the centre in all the parts of it.'[16]

In the technical language of the schools, the second theory
would seem to be a 'realist' theory of the universal as being the
common qualities present in the members of a class of particulars.
It would be nothing new, it would be found not made. Yet Locke
repeatedly asserts that general ideas are made by the mind.
'General and universal belong not to the real existence of things

45

but are the inventions and creatures of the understanding made
by it for its own use.'[17] Locke continues in this passage to explain
how this can be by referring to the first theory of general ideas –
that a general idea is a particular idea 'signifying' or standing for
other particular ideas, and adding that this relation of 'signifying'
depends on the mind. If there were no minds the whiteness of milk
would not stand for or signify the whitenesses of chalk and snow.
All that exists independently of the mind would be the similarities
between these whitenesses. General ideas are 'the workmanship of
the understanding but have their foundation in the similitude of
things'.[18] But on the second theory this 'similitude' of particular
ideas has been analysed as the possession of a group of common
qualities which can be separately considered and, thus abstracted,
are a general idea. How, on this view, can the general idea be said
to be the creature of the understanding, when it is in fact the
group of common qualities shared by a number of particulars?

Stillingfleet forcibly put this difficulty to Locke. 'Peter and
James and John are all true and real men; but what is it which
makes them so? Is it the attributing of a general name to them?
No certainly, but that the true and real essence of a man is in every
one of them.'[19] Locke's answer seems to concede Stillingfleet's
point: 'How . . . are we certain that they are men but only by our
senses finding those properties in them which answer to the
abstract complex idea which is in our minds.'[20] The mind 'in
making its complex ideas of substance only follows nature and
puts no ideas together which are not supposed to have a union in
nature . . . men, observing certain qualities always joined and
existing together, therein copied nature, and of ideas so united
made their complex ones of substance, etc.'[21]

How then can Locke continue to maintain that general ideas
are the work of the mind? He gives, in various places, a number of
different answers. They centre round his distinction between
ideas and reality, and his belief that the real nature of objects is
unknown to us. 'There is an internal constitution of things on
which their properties depend. . . . There are also complex ideas
or combinations of these properties in men's minds to which they
annex specific names'.[22] And Stillingfleet had laid himself open
to this by making the same distinction.

This difference [between nominal and real essence] doth not
depend upon the complex ideas of substance, whereby men

46

arbitrarily join modes together in their minds; for let them mistake in the complication of their ideas, either in leaving out or in putting in what doth not belong to them; and let their ideas be what they please, the real essence of a man, and a horse and a tree are just what they were . . . these real essences are unchangeable.[23]

So, for Stillingfleet too, men's ideas are their own making. Locke comments:

For example, let your lordship's idea, to which you annex the sign man, be a rational animal; let another man's be a rational animal of such a shape; let a third man's idea be of an animal of such a size and shape leaving out rationality . . . it is plain that everyone of these will call his a man, as well as your lordship, and yet it is as plain that man, as standing for all these distinct complex ideas, cannot be supposed to have the same internal constitution, i.e. the same real essence. The truth is, every distinct abstract idea with a name to it, makes a real distinct kind, whatever the real essence (*which we know not of any of them*) be.[24] [My italics.]

Here is Locke's first argument to show that abstract general ideas are mind-made. The mere fact that they are distinct from real qualities would not alone be enough, for Locke thinks our ideas of substance are *caused* by the operation of these substances and would not then be mind-dependent. The first argument, then, is that different people make different *selections* of characteristics to distinguish kinds or classes of particulars. There are two points concerning the validity of this argument. First, it explains variations in the meaning attached to the word 'man', but does not show that the group of qualities to which any individual attaches the word (e.g. rational biped) is itself mind-dependent. Indeed, as the final sentence from the passage last quoted admits, 'every distinct abstract idea makes a real distinct kind'. Secondly, as noted above, the solution applies to substantives such as 'man', 'horse', but not so obviously to adjectives such as 'rational'. The word 'man' may represent an individual's selection of characteristics, but it is not so clear that 'rational' does too. It may, perhaps, if it is a complex idea; but certainly a simple idea, such as whiteness, cannot do so. So some general ideas cannot be shown to be mind-dependent by this argument.

47

Moreover it would seem that it is not only the ideas of the constituent qualities of a group that is independent of the mind. So is their *coexistence*. 'Though the mind of man in making its complex ideas of substances never puts together any that do not really or are not supposed to coexist and so it truly borrows that union from nature, yet the number it combines depends upon the various care, industry or fancy of him that makes it.'[25]

Despite these difficulties, Locke is dealing here with an important and interesting problem. Classification systems are to some extent arbitrary; and the study of taxonomy deals with the most effective and illuminating methods of classifying any particular subject-matter, (e.g. plants or insects).

The second argument urged by Locke to show that general ideas are mind-made is the occurrence of debated or doubtful specimens. It has been 'doubted whether the foetus born of a woman were a man' [sc. in the case of a monstrous birth]; and 'the frequent productions of monsters in all the species of animals, and of changelings and other strange issues of human birth carry with them difficulties not possible to consist with this hypothesis' [the hypothesis of 'real essences' or fixed independent natural kinds].[26] This is a sound argument. Whatever characteristics one may take as the defining characteristics of a species there will be instances which lack them and yet cannot be attributed to another species.

A third argument arises from the existence of borderline or intermediate cases which we do not know where to place, as between two kinds.

In all the visible corporeal world we see no chasms or gaps. All quite down from us the descent is by easy steps . . . that in each remove differ very little, one from another. There are fishes that have wings . . . there are birds . . . whose blood is as cold as fishes and their flesh so like in taste that the scrupulous are allowed them on fish-days . . . amphibious animals link the terrestrial and aquatic together; . . . there are some brutes that seem to have as much knowledge and reason as some that are called men; . . . everywhere the several species are linked together and differ but in almost insensible degrees.[27]

This argument too is effective and unanswerable.

Locke then makes a good case against the independent reality

48

of essences or universals. He sums up his view in the *Essay*
(iii vi 30–36) very effectively. Nature makes things similar in all
sorts of ways and men take occasion from these similarities to
range individuals into sorts. But the arrangements are ours, and,
for convenience, they often rest on a few outward and obvious
similarities. The aim of this sorting is convenience of communica-
tion; 'therefore these boundaries of species are as men and not as
Nature makes them, if at least there are in nature any such
prefixed bounds'.[28]

There are two kinds of general ideas to which the preceding
arguments do not apply: artificial objects and mixed modes.
Artificial objects are made to specifications known to the maker
and there is therefore less room for doubt. This is a sound point,
but Locke seems mistaken when he says that the essence of an
artefact is 'the determinate figure of its sensible parts'.[29] This will
be clear if an attempt is made to determine the 'figure' of bed, or
chair, or tobacco pipe. The 'essence' of an artefact is its purpose or
use. Mixed modes are 'scattered and independent ideas put together by the mind'[30] and can be 'made by the mind without any
pattern to fashion it by'.[31] This also is a genuine exception to the
main theory, though of course, as Locke points out, the simple
ideas into which any such mixed mode can be analysed must come
ultimately from sensation or reflection.

Later Developments Recent discussions of the problems raised by
general terms have built on Locke's first solution (which is also
that of Berkeley and Hume) so far as the classification of features
of the world of experience are concerned. The easiest example in
which to see the start of this development is 'colour'. 'Red' is the
term applicable to a *range* of colours which have what is called 'a
family resemblance' to each other. On Locke's second theory, one
would have to say that crimson was a complex idea including the
general idea red and the specific idea which differentiates crimson
from cherry. And the general idea red would itself be complex
because it would include the more general idea colour with the
specific feature which differentiates red from blue. It seems obvious
that this internal complexity is a myth. The very natural assumption that, when two entities resemble each other, this resemblance
can be analysed into points of identity and points of difference has
to be rejected. Resemblance is an unanalysable relation. It might
be thought that, in that case, there would be continuous grada-
tions so that any selection of a 'resembling family' would be

c*

49

arbitrary. The spectrum is a continuous band of colours. Red may be taken as a centre shading off into orange and purple; or purple as a centre shading off into red and blue. These two ranges would overlap. But sometimes there seems good reason to take a particular instance as a 'centre' and to regard the resembling cases as in various degrees divergent from it. This central case is called the 'paradigm case'. It and the other cases will not have features common to them all but some of them will have some features in common with the paradigm case. Those who put forward these theories would no doubt make the same exceptions as does Locke. Artefacts have a genuine common feature in their purpose or use. And it is possible for the mind to attach its own meaning to terms so that unanalysable resemblances and divergence from paradigm cases do not arise. (This may occur in law or in pure mathematics.)

6 Knowledge of Minds

In previous chapters two points about our knowledge of the mind have emerged. First, that we have simple ideas of reflection as well as of sensation and that in Locke 'reflection' means introspection, 'when the mind turns its view inward upon itself and contemplates its own actions'.[1] We noted that 'reflection' should not be confused with reasoning, pondering, considering, thinking, with which its modern usage identifies it (chapter 1, p. 18).

The second point already noted is that Locke says that the first simple idea of reflection to occur to us is that of thinking; and he treats sensation, memory, reverie, reasoning, judging, volition and knowledge as 'modes of thinking'. On this account, thinking would be not merely the *first* but the *only* simple idea of reflection and *all* the so-called mental activities listed would be its modes. Some difficulties of this view are noted above (p. 19).

Locke does not maintain it consistently. Chapter VI of Book II of the *Essay* is headed "Of simple *Ideas* of Reflection", and the plural 'Ideas' is borne out by the text (para. 2) which says: 'The two great and principal actions of the mind are . . . perception or thinking and volition or willing . . . of some of the modes of these simple ideas of reflection, such as are remembrance, discerning, reasoning, judging, knowledge, faith etc., I shall have occasion to speak hereafter.' Thus, on this view, there are two simple ideas of reflection and all mental activities are modes of one or the other. Locke also shows some doubt about the whole approach. He says: 'Perception is the first *and simplest* idea we have from reflection'[2] [my italics]; and, again, perception 'being distinct from all other modifications of thinking furnishes the mind with a distinct idea which we call sensation'. After considering other mental activities,

51

he adds: 'These are some of those various modes of thinking which the mind may observe in itself and so have as distinct ideas of as it hath of white and red, a square or a circle'.[3] But white and red are simple ideas. In fact, the whole distinction between simple ideas and modes here breaks down. The only way to maintain a view like Locke's would be this. Let us start with sensation. Besides being aware of colours, I am aware of seeing as a mental activity. But it might be argued that *as a mental activity* seeing is not *introspectively distinguishable* from hearing. The association of the two activities with eyes and ears is learned independently and not introspectively given. What I know by reflection is that I am *aware* of colours and *aware* of sounds. The awareness is the common mental feature, the difference lies in the objects.

This could then be extended to other cases. Remembering is awareness of past events, reasoning is awareness of necessary connections between ideas. But Locke does not accept this solution. He thinks in some cases (sensation) the mind is passive and in others (reasoning) the mind is active, and this activity is directly inspected not inferred. And he also argues that the mind has *distinct ideas* of all its mental states. 'There are several actions of men's minds that they are conscious to themselves of performing, as willing, believing, knowing, etc., which they have so particular a sense of that they can distinguish them one from another; or else they could not say when they willed, when they believed, and when they knew anything.'[4] So the notion that seeing is a complex idea made up of the simple idea of consciousness and the simple ideas of colours, and that reasoning is a complex idea made up of the simple idea of consciousness and the complex idea of necessarily connected simple ideas (triangle, angle, three, two right), will not do. Locke should have held that there are as many simple ideas of reflection as there are discernible, distinct and not further analysable introspected mental states, and that thinking and willing are abstract general ideas, not given but made by the mind.

Embedded in this difficult discussion is one particular confusion which Locke himself notes but to which he falls victim, that is his confusion between thinking as a general term covering all mental states and thinking as equivalent to reasoning. One example of this confusion occurs in his long attack on the Cartesian view that 'the soul always thinks'. Descartes had held that the essential nature of the soul was thinking; and therefore, since the soul had a continual existence, there could be no time when the soul existed but was not thinking. Locke challenges this with the evidence of dreamless sleep. He urges, reasonably enough, that it is odd that, if there is no dreamless sleep, so few dreams are remembered. And he goes on to argue that the thoughts of a sleeping man ought to be the most rational whereas the images of dreams are fleeting and useless.

> It is hardly to be conceived that our infinitely wise Creator should make so admirable a faculty as the power of thinking, that faculty which comes nearest the excellency of his own incomprehensible being, to be so idly and uselessly employed at least a fourth part of its time here as to think constantly without remembering any of those thoughts, without doing any good to itself or others or being in any way useful to any other part of the creation.[5]

He goes on to argue that the dreams we do remember are 'extravagant and incoherent' and 'little conformable to the perfection and order of a rational being'. Thus 'the soul when separate from the body acts less rationally than when conjoined with it. If its separate thoughts be less rational, then these men must say that the soul owes the perfection of rational thinking to the body.'[6] Here the essence of the soul is obviously held to be 'rational thinking'. But the issue is whether there are periods of total unconsciousness and mere thinking = consciousness, any of whose 'modes', memory, reverie, and presumably dream, would qualify to fill the gaps. As against Descartes, however, the argument, with this confusion in it, may still carry weight, for Descartes himself fell into the same confusion. For the all-inclusive use of 'think' compare 'what am I? A thinking thing, it has been said. And what is a thinking thing? It is a thing that doubts, understands, conceives, affirms, denies, wills, refuses, that imagines also perceives.'[7] 'I find in myself diverse faculties of thinking that have each their special mode: for example I possess the faculties of imagining and perceiving. . . .'[8] For the restricted use by which 'think' means 'reason'. 'I am therefore a thinking thing, that is, a mind, understanding or reason.'[9]

Locke is aware of the danger of speaking of perception as 'thinking' or a kind of thinking. He says 'perception . . . is the first and simplest idea we have from reflection and is by some called

53

thinking in general; though thinking in the propriety of the English tongue signifies that sort of operation in the mind about its ideas wherein the mind is active'.[10]

Reflection or introspection, Locke notes, does not occur until the mind has developed. Children are too much concerned with the world around them, as revealed by sensation, to attend to their own mental states, and this continues to be true of most men throughout adult life. So men 'seldom make any considerable attention on what passes within them till they come to be of riper years and some scarce ever at all'.[11] There are two apparent contradictions to this account of introspection as late and rare.

First, there is the question of pain and pleasure. When they are first discussed, they are said to come into the mind (like the ideas of existence, power and succession) both by sensation and by reflection.[12] But Locke seems to correct this later when he says: 'By pleasure and pain I must be understood to mean of body or mind as they are commonly distinguished, though in truth they be only different constitutions of the mind.'[13] And this correction seems fully justified. The distinction between 'bodily' pain and mental 'distress' is a distinction due to their causes and not to their nature as experiences. Pain and pleasure, then, being always mental states should be 'ideas of reflection'. But they are not rare and late experiences. The reason for these exceptions perhaps lies in Locke's argument that the receiving of ideas of reflection requires attention, and our attention is normally directed elsewhere. But it is difficult not to attend to pleasure and pain (though not impossible, as the disappearance of toothache during the daytime shows). 'A man on the rack is not at liberty to lay by the idea of pain and divert himself with other contemplations.'[14]

The other exception to the view that reflection occurs rarely and late in life arises when Locke on two separate occasions seems to argue that we are *at all times* conscious of our own mental processes. The first occasion is his attack on the view that thinking is incessant. He instances (as noted above) periods of dreamless sleep and has to meet the suggestion that during these periods we think but are not conscious of thinking. Locke says that it is unintelligible to say that anything thinks without being conscious of it or perceiving that it does so. Those who talk thus 'may with as much reason . . . say that a man is always hungry but that he does not always feel it, whereas hunger consists in that very sensation, as thinking consists in being conscious that one thinks. . . . Conscious-

54

ness is the perception of what passes in a man's own mind.'[15] Locke is here arguing that, whenever we think (perceive, imagine etc.), we are conscious of thinking (perceiving, imagining etc.). The same view recurs on a second occasion when he is discussing personal identity. He says a person is 'a thinking, intelligent being, that has reason and reflection and can consider itself as the same thinking thing in different times and places, which it does only by that consciousness which is inseparable from thinking and, as it seems to me, essential to it: it being impossible for anyone to perceive without perceiving that he does perceive. When we see, hear, smell, taste, feel, meditate, or will anything, we know that we do so.'[16]

There is a special reason why, in this context, Locke should hold that we are always aware of our own mental activities. He bases personal identity on memory. Now memory is always recollection of *my own* doings and sufferings. I may say that I remember the coronation of Edward VII or the old Euston Station, but strictly speaking what I remember is *receiving* my coronation mug or *seeing* the old station. Yet it would be odd if I recalled seeing the station, but at the time I was not aware of seeing the station (but only of the sensation, or ideas of sensation themselves). 'As far as any intelligent being can repeat the idea of any past action with the same consciousness it had of it at first and with the same consciousness as it has of any present action, so far it is the same personal self.'[17]

A final problem about reflection is its reliability; Locke sharply distinguished ideas of sensation from the qualities of things. What would he say about ideas of reflection? They are introduced with the same language as ideas of sensation. 'He that contemplates the operations of his mind cannot but have plain and clear ideas of them.'[18] Here is the distinction between the ideas and the operations, as between ideas and real qualities in the case of sensation. But the passage quoted above on the consciousness that accompanies all our perception suggests a direct awareness of the mental operations themselves. Nowhere is there any suggestion, as there is with secondary qualities, that the ideas we have by introspection fail to reveal the states of our own mind. At the end of the *Essay* Locke says: 'Since the things the mind contemplates are none of them *beside itself* present to the understanding, it is necessary that something else, as a sign or representation of the thing it considers, should be present to it; and these are ideas.'[19]

It might be said that what is certain is the *existence* of our own minds and not any particular state of them. This would seem to be confirmed by the section heading of iv ix 3; "Our knowledge of our own existence is intuitive". But, in that section, the argument is that our knowledge of our own existence is as certain as that of our mental states. 'If I know I feel pain it is evident that I have as certain perception of my own existence as of the existence of the pain I feel.' Locke does not show how these two certainties are connected. The answer must be in the intellectual necessity linking quality with substance. Pain (like the red colour of a cherry) implies something to which the pain belongs. And this is a reality not merely an idea if the quality in question is real (as pain is and as the red colour of a cherry is not). So Locke does not hold that we can be certain of the *existence* of our own selves, though our awareness of the operations of the self is uncertain and introspection fallible.

Therefore the representative theory of perception applies only to the world outside us, including of course the minds of other people.

These conclusions have been under continuous assault in recent times.

First, the place of introspection in knowledge of one's own operations and feelings, has been reduced to a minimum or, as by behaviourist psychology, eliminated altogether. Much of my knowledge of myself comes, as does my knowledge of other people, from consideration of my own conduct. The suggestion that I can and should think before I speak is properly met by the retort 'How can I know what I think until I hear what I say?' And if it is still insisted that I can think without expressing my thoughts aloud, these unspoken thoughts are identified with suppressed or rudimentary speech-behaviour with 'sensori-motor processes in the larynx'. But, despite these attacks, there still seems a place, if a reduced one, for introspection and for experiences, such as pain, which are irreducible to physical expression in cries of anguish or to physiological behaviour such as cringes or twitches.

The other line of attack would maintain that introspection is fallible. The evidence of the psychoanalysts is the main source here. But ordinary experience often justifies similar conclusions. We see jealousy masquerading as righteous indignation, fear as bravado. The problem, however, is how exactly these situations are to be described. That suggested by the attack on introspection

56

would be: 'He is not really indignant but jealous. He does not really feel aggressive he feels frightened.' Now, in the latter case, this may well be accurate. His conduct may be aggressive but his feeling is fear. But this throws no doubt on introspection. The 'masquerade' is a physical front for an inappropriate psychological state. But if the agent would honestly describe his feeling as fear or indignation, how can we say it is 'really' something quite different? An alternative description would admit that the feeling he claims to have is real but that it has no adequate *ground* and that its *cause* is something quite different from what would normally be the case. Groundless fears are fears all the same; and 'referred pains' are still felt as 'in the shoulder' no matter how much evidence is given that their cause is in a heart condition.

One's own knowledge of the existence and states and characteristics of other people receives very little attention by Locke. It is presumably attained by sensation since this is the only alternative to intuition and demonstration, and this would mean by perception of the bodies of other people and inference (from my own experience of my own pains etc.) to their inner feelings and from their speech to their inner ideas.[20] But in the one passage where he raises this issue he says: 'The having ideas of spirits does not make us know that any such things do exist without us or that there are any finite spirits or any other spiritual beings but the eternal God. We have ground from revelation and several other reasons to believe with assurance that there are such creatures but our senses not being able to discover them we want the means of knowing their particular existences.'[21] But he does not tell us what these other reasons are, and the whole passage seems concerned rather with incorporeal finite spirits (angels or devils) than with other people.

Locke's
if can't be
coext. → different ✓✓
inferences can't be
co beginning → different.

7 Personal Identity; and Mind-and-Body

In the long and intricate chapter (II xxvii) entitled "Of Identity and Diversity", which Locke added in the second edition of the *Essay*, he discusses the problem how we come to believe in the continued existence of persons and the criteria for saying someone is the same person as he was days or years ago. I shall in this chapter review his discussion of personal identity, and conclude it with some comments on his references to the mind-body relationship.

mind
body
inferences

(i) *Personal Identity*

different ways can't be
spatio temporally
coextensive =

Locke begins the discussion with some general comments on identity. Two things cannot be in the same place at the same time; from which he appears to believe that it follows that two things cannot have the same beginning in time. These considerations are difficult to relate to the problem of continuous existence. The two 'things' which cannot be in the same place at the same time might both be evanescent and not continuing entities. The second test does seem to concern continuing existences. But it begs the question. Suppose I ask whether the pen with which I am now writing is the pen which I bought five years ago. I should have to establish the beginning in time of each of these pens. But to establish that the pen I am writing with 'began' in a certain factory in 1967 is already to require criteria for continued existence.

presuppose
continuity

Locke then goes on to preface his discussion of the identity of persons by some brief remarks on other types of identity; the identity of 'bodies' and the identity of vegetables and animals.

58

Use Jenkins pp. instead

He says the *principium individuationis* (principle of individuality) is 'existence itself' determining a being to a particular time and place. But this again does not face the problem of continued identity and Locke seems to fall back into the tautology 'A is A'. When he does mention continued existence, he says: 'Let us suppose an atom, i.e. a continued body under one immutable superfices existing in a determined time and place: it is evident that considered in any instant of its existence it is in that instant the same with itself . . . and so must continue as long as its existence is continued; for so long it will be the same and no other.'[1] It is impossible to give a clear meaning to this; but it seems to be groping towards the conception of individuality as spatio-temporal continuity. I say that the pen I am writing with is the pen I bought five years ago if there is an unbroken spatio-temporal continuity between the pen now and the pen in that shop. It is to be noted that, for this condition to be satisfied, it is not necessary that the pen should have 'one immutable superfices' (shape and size), though pens normally do. My wallet which I found in the garden shrunken and warped is the one I lost; and this means that I believe that, if I had been able to observe it continuously from that day to this, I should have seen no gaps in its history; I should have seen it shrinking and warping. In fact, what I do observe is not the timeless present state of things but short sections of their continuous life. That the pen with which I write 'p' is the same as the pen with which I write 'e' and 'n' is directly observed. I can slice a three-dimensional oblong cake into thin slices but each slice is still a three-dimensional object. A cake does not consist of a pile of two-dimensional surfaces. So I can slice the life of a pen, a four-dimensional object, into short slices (the pen with which I write the word 'pen') but this slice is still a four-dimensional object with a time dimension (.03 sec.) as well as the spatial dimensions. When I cannot observe the continued spatio-temporal existence of an object, I have to fall back on other evidence (similarity, situation etc.) which will always be inconclusive. And, of course, a conjurer can make me believe I have observed the spatio-temporal continuity of an object when I have not.

Locke goes on to point out that a mere heap or aggregate of atoms remains the same if the atoms of which it is composed remain the same. But if any are removed or replaced it is no longer the same heap.

He then goes on to consider living bodies and here is worried by the recognition that the material of which a vegetable or animal is composed need not remain the same. Clearly a grown oak contains more atoms than a sapling and a lopped oak less than a grown oak; yet the sapling the grown tree and the lopped tree can all be the same tree. What then constitutes the identity of the tree? Locke's answer is that the parts of an oak are organised to receive and distribute nourishment – the wood, the bark, the leaves etc. So it is one plant because it has 'an organisation of parts in one coherent body'.[2]

Now clearly this is an important admission from such an atomistic analyst as Locke. The unity of an organism is different from the unity of a heap, and the unity of an organism is that of parts contributing to a single purpose or purposes. But this by itself does nothing to answer the question of *continued* identity. Locke finds a similar principle of unity in a machine, and this example will again show the difficulty. The fact that the various parts of my pen are so arranged as to supply a steady flow of ink at the point does nothing to show whether this is the same pen that I bought four years ago.

It might be urged that the interacting parts cannot be understood at a single moment of time. The process of digestion and nourishment is a *process*, and the contribution of the parts to it so spread through time. Thus the growth of the oak must be seen in relation to the *previous* processes of ingestion and assimilation; and it is the same oak as it was at the beginning of these processes because they contribute to its *subsequent* development. Organisation is not simply a relation between part and whole, but between present and future. This too is an important point. But it also is insufficient to establish identity. For I could observe ingestion *and* assimilation *and* growth in sequence and still ask whether this is the same tree (as a botanist might, who is growing twelve specimens for systematic comparison). The difficulty is only too obvious in Locke's own text:

That being then one plant which has such an organisation of parts in one coherent body, partaking of one common life, it continues to be the same plant so long as it partakes of the same life, though that life be communicated to new particles of matter vitally united to the living plant, in a like continued organisation, conformable to that sort of plants. For this organisation

60

being at any one instant in that collection of matter, is in that particular concrete distinguished from all other is that individual life, which existing constantly from that moment both forwards and backwards in the same continuity of insensibly succeeding parts united to the living body of the plant it has that identity which makes the same plant and all the parts of it parts of the same plant during all the time that they exist united in that continued organisation.[3]

The principle of identity is still spatio-temporal continuity (the 'continuity of insensibly succeeding parts'). When this continuity is not directly observed, we cannot (as in the case of the pen) fall back on the evidence of similarity because the sapling and the fully-grown tree are quite dissimilar. We know, however, how oak saplings develop into oaks and we say 'this is the tree I planted' on the basis of this evidence. But, just as similarity in pens is very inadequate evidence for identity, so similar history ('conformable to that sort of plant') is also inadequate. My sapling might have died and some one else have planted, later that same year, another oak sapling in its place.

The identity of an animal, says Locke, is not much different. It is 'one continued body all of whose organised parts are repaired, increased, or diminished by a constant addition or separation of insensible parts'.[4]

For most practical purposes the identity of a man is on the same basis, though to identity of body (which is spatio-temporal continuity) may be added personal identity. 'For it is not the idea of a thinking or rational being alone that makes the idea of a man in most people's sense, but of a body so and so shaped joined to it; and, if that be the idea of man, the same successive body not shifted all at once must, as well as the same immaterial spirit, go to the making of the same man.' Spatio-temporal continuity here again is the criterion for 'same body' – 'same successive body not shifted all at once'. Locke is uncertain whether to make personal identity essential to the identity of a man (embryo and madman causing difficulty here).

He then goes on to examine personal identity. Locke's basis for continued personal identity is memory. I am identified with the person who experienced x if I can remember experiencing x. 'As far as any intelligent being can repeat the idea of any past action with the same consciousness it had of it at first and with the same consciousness as it has of any present action; so far it is the same personal self.'[6]

The difficulty, as Locke says, in this theory is forgetfulness. There are some experiences we cannot remember, and it might seem that the only evidence that we are the same persons as had those experiences would be the indirect evidence that our bodies were present on these occasions (as confirmed, for example, by our diaries and the memories of other people). There is also the difficulty that, on Locke's view, there are periods of dreamless sleep when we have no experiences to remember. It could of course be argued that, if I can remember an experience in 1902, I am identical with the child who had that experience, and a continued identity from 1902 to 1972 will cross all those gaps created by experiences which I cannot remember or periods when I had no experiences at all. Locke does not argue thus, and seems even prepared to consider that periods of dreamless sleep are periods in which I, as an immaterial substance, cease for the time being to exist.

A further difficulty Locke notices is the possibility of pseudo-memory, when the mind might remember 'what it never did and what was perhaps done by some other agent'. Locke sees no logical ground for rejecting this and appeals to the goodness of God who would not allow one person to feel responsible for what another had done, especially as this 'draws reward and punishment'.[7] Locke comes to the conclusion that, if the same body were associated with two sets of experiences $A^1, A^2, A^3, \ldots B^1, B^2, B^3$, such that all earlier As could be recalled by later As and earlier Bs by later Bs, but no B by an A or vice versa, then the body would be inhabited by two different persons. 'If it is possible for the same man to have distinct incommunicable consciousness at different times it is past doubt that the same man would at different times make different persons.'[8] When Jekyll and Hyde multiple-personality situations have been reported from real life, the dissociation has not normally been of this extreme kind. In the classic case of Sally Beauchamp, BI and BII could not recall the experiences of Sally or of each other, but Sally could recall the experiences of both of them as well as her own[9]

The later development of these arguments is lively and continuous. From the immense literature on them three specimens may be extracted. Locke's theory is considered by A. G. N. Flew in "Locke and the Problem of Personal Identity";[10] the connection between personal identity and memory by H. P. Grice in "Personal Identity";[11] and the Spatio-Temporal Continuity criterion in connection with personal identity by D. Wiggins.[12]

(ii) The Mind–Body Relationship

A problem arising from Locke's discussions is the equally perennial issue of the relation between mind and body. Locke's references to this issue are few and unconstructive. They are bedevilled by his confusions on substances. He argues, in the section on personal identity, that identity of consciousness (with the memory criterion) does not imply identity of substance, though he thinks it is 'probable' that a single consciousness is annexed to one individual immaterial substance.[13] Yet he also speaks of the mind as located in space;[14] and, in his final review of the question, he even regards it as possible that God has endowed matter with the capacity to think,[15] which would involve a single type of substance, and would avoid the problems of the relation of mind and body. This suggestion was naturally taken by his critics, and particularly by Stillingfleet, as a serious threat to Christian doctrine and particularly to the doctrine of the immortality of the soul. Stillingfleet says: 'The great ends of religion and morality are best served by proofs of the immortality of the soul from its nature and properties; and which I think prove it immaterial. I do not question whether God can give immortality to a material substance; but I say it takes off very much from the evidence of immortality if it depends wholly upon God's giving that which of its own nature it is not capable of.'[16] Locke's reply[17] is very effective. He points our first that he had said that in his own view it was probable that the soul was an immaterial substance. But it could not be certainly demonstrated that matter could not think. If it could, let Stillingfleet provide the demonstration and Locke would rejoice that what he thought probable could be shown to be certain. But he could not see why God should not endow certain material bodies with the power of thought as he has endowed certain of them with life, spontaneous movement, sensation and propagation. Moreover how would the doctrine of the immortality of the soul be helped by its immateriality, when Christians are committed to a belief in the immortality of a material body (the resurrection body)? If it is difficult to conceive how a material body can think, it is no less difficult to conceive how an immaterial soul and a material body can interact. And

63

the view that the theory of immortality requires a belief that the soul is immaterial is brought into doubt when it is observed that theories which rely on this connection (such as Plato's) have to believe in the soul's pre-existence, which is no part of Christian doctrine.

The mind–body problem has an even longer and livelier history than the problem of personal identity. On the whole it would probably be fair to say that the general tendency is towards a 'single substance' theory, as adumbrated by Locke in the suggestion that matter might think. An effective presentation of this solution and of the difficulties of the 'two-substance' view is G. Ryle's *The Concept of Mind*.

8 The Freedom of the Will

The second great debate, arising from the discussion of human personality, to which Locke gave extended and careful treatment was that concerning free will.

In discussing the idea of power Locke had noted that the powers of the mind are usually called 'faculties'. He had warned his readers against the common tendency, encouraged by ordinary language, to suppose that such faculties as understanding and will are 'real beings in the soul that performed those actions of understanding and volition'.[1] He goes on to argue that the question whether a man's will is free or not is an improper question. It should be whether or not a man is free.[2] His first account of freedom is that a man is free if he is able to give effect to 'the preference or direction of his own mind',[3] or to refrain from doing so. This is freedom from external constraint. A man in chains is not free. But it is to be noted that the restraint need not be external in the sense of being exercised by factors outside the body of the agent. Palsy or St Vitus's Dance are equally causes of loss of freedom.[4] So too is the pain of torture or a 'boisterous passion'.[5] It is also to be noted that *both* alternatives, to do or to refrain, must be open to the agent if he is to be free. A man who prefers to stay in prison acts voluntarily but not freely, if he would be unable to leave the prison if he so wished. This is so far satisfactory, though the problem of delimiting the 'boisterous passion' is a difficult one. So the formula for freedom is: 'I can do x if I choose or I can refrain from doing x if I choose.' But what about my choice! Can I choose otherwise than I do? Locke first makes clear that I cannot avoid making *some* choice or other. 'A man that is walking to whom it is proposed to give off walking is not at liberty whether he will determine himself to walk or give off walking or not: he must necessarily prefer one or the other of them, walking or not walking . . . the mind has not a power to forbear willing.'[6]

But the next question is the crucial one for a free-will theory: 'Whether a man be at liberty to will which of the two he pleases, motion or rest.'[7] What then determines the choice? Locke's answer is 'uneasiness'.[8] though strictly speaking uneasiness determines only a change of direction of the will. 'The motive for continuing in the same state or action is the present satisfaction in it.'[9] When it is said that the motive for all actions is pleasure either present or anticipated, Locke argues rightly that, while a present pleasure can be a motive for continuing in the same condition, an anticipated pleasure is a desired pleasure and desire itself is accompanied by uneasiness or dissatisfaction and it is this uneasiness which actually drives a man to act. In particular, since a man may have many conscious desires, it is the 'most pressing',[10] most important and urgent',[11] 'greatest and most pressing'[12] uneasiness which determines the choice. So far, then, Locke is a psychological determinist, whose specific explanation of human action is egoistic hedonism. (Locke's hedonism is discussed more fully below in connection with his moral theory; see chapter 12.) Along these lines it is difficult to see how Locke can retain any freedom at all. He has agreed that palsy can stop a man from being able to move and he has added that pain or fury can also stop a man from being able not to move. But would not this apply to whatever was 'the greatest and most pressing uneasiness'?

Locke himself, however, provides a loophole which leads him to a completely different conception of freedom. There are occasions when the most pressing uneasiness does not determine choice. It does so

> for the most part but not always. For the mind having in most cases, as is evident in experience, the power to suspend the execution and satisfaction of any of its desires, and so all, one after another, is at liberty to consider the objects of them, examine them on all sides and weigh them with others. In this lies the liberty man has and from the not using of it right comes all that variety of mistakes, errors and faults which we run into in the conduct of our lives.[13]

The 'consideration' to which Locke refers is a judgment of the good or evil of what we are going to do. Again, however, once this process of examination is completed, action is completely determined by 'the last result of a fair examination'. Locke argues vigorously that any supposition that we might be free to choose any alternative to this 'result' is indefensible.

> A perfect indifference in the mind, not determinable by its last judgment of good or evil that is thought to attend its choice would be so far from being an advantage and excellency of any intellectual nature that it would be as great an imperfection as the want of indifferency to act or not to act till determined by the will, would be an imperfection on the other side.[14]

'God himself cannot choose what is not good.'[15] So 'the certainer such determination is the greater is the perfection'. Locke hesitates to say that *only* a decision taken after such full examination and determined by its results is a free decision, though he comes close to this in several places. 'The stronger ties we have to an unalterable pursuit of happiness in general which is our greatest good . . . the more are we free from any necessary determination of our will to any particular action.'[16] This is the theory familiar from Kant that only moral action is free. When we act immorally we are the slaves of our passions, subject to 'necessary determination to particular actions'.

But Locke also returns to the view that the basic freedom is not that of acting on a fair examination of good or evil but that of being able to suspend the activity of any desire and to do the examination required. (Compare the quotation above, p. 66; 'In this lies the liberty man has'.)

> This is the hinge on which turns the liberty of intellectual beings in their constant endeavours after and a steady prosecution of true felicity, that they can suspend this prosecution in particular cases, till they had looked before them and informed themselves whether that particular thing, which is then proposed or desired, lie in the way to their main end, and make a real part of that which is their greatest good.[17]

It would seem here that the decision to suspend the operation of a desire and to examine what its results would be in terms of general good – that this decision is the perfect example of free will. The suspension and the subsequent examination would not seem to be motivated by any uneasinesss but to be something we just decide (or do not decide) to do and to go on doing until we decide to stop. But Locke blocks this loophole himself. The passage quoted immediately above continues:

> For the inclination and tendency of their nature to happiness is an obligation and motive to them to take care not to mistake or miss it; and so necessarily puts them upon caution, deliberation and wariness in the direction of their particular actions, which are the means to obtain it. Whatever necessity determines to the pursuit of real bliss, the same necessity with the same force establishes suspense, deliberation and scrutiny of each successive desire . . . I desire it may be well considered whether the great inlet and exercise of all the liberty men have, are capable of, or can be useful to them and that whereon depends the turn of their actions does not lie in this, that they can suspend their desires and stop them from determining their wills to any action till they have duly and fairly examined the good and evil of it.[18]

Thus the motivation of the suspension and examination is our desire for the maximum happiness and this desire *necessitates* these operations. Yet the language of free will creeps back again. When Locke remembers that often enough we do not suspend and examine. He says God 'knows our frailty, pities our weakness and requires of us no more than we are able to do'. But since restraint of passion to make possible calm examination is necessary for true happiness,

> it is in this we should employ our chief care and endeavours. In this we should take pains to suit the relish of our minds to the true intrinsic good or ill that is in things, and not permit an allowed or supposed possible great and weighty good to slip out of our thoughts . . . till, by a due consideration of its true worth, we have formed appetites in our minds suitable to it and made ourselves uneasy in the want of it.[19]

Here it is suggested that, if we are not inclined to look before and after, we can take pains to develop this tendency, or again that, though insufficiently attracted by some 'weighty good', we can by our own efforts develop a desire for it.

These views seem, as Locke claims, to be based on our own experience and they do appear to throw doubt on the complete psychological determinism which is the main thread in his argument. This is further discussed in chapter 12, pp. 122–6.

The issue of freedom is important because, as Locke sees, it is bound up with the questions of responsibility and justice. We do not punish lunatics because they cannot help doing what they do. But if every act a man does is necessitated by the strength of his uneasiness at the time and if even his 'suspensions' and 'examinations' in the search for the true good are necessitated by the desire for true happiness, then he could never have helped doing what he did. When Locke faces this issue he again reverts to the indeterminism noted above.

> And here we may see how it comes to pass that a man may justly incur punishment though it be certain that in all the particular actions that he wills he does, and necessarily does will that which he then judges to be good; . . . because by a too hasty choice of his own making, he has imposed on himself wrong measures of good and evil . . . he has vitiated his own palate and must be answerable to himself for the sickness and death that follows from it. . . . If the neglect or abuse of the liberty he had to examine what would really and truly make for his happiness, misleads him, the miscarriages that follow on it must be imputed to his own election.[20]

The problem of free will like that of personal identity remained a permanent crux for philosophers. Later writers unanimously applauded Locke's attack on the faculty fallacy, and his insistence that men not wills are free. The view that freedom consists simply in lack of impediments has had a regular following. For them 'I could have done x (though I didn't)' is to be interpreted as 'I could (or even I would) have done x if I had wished'. This is compatible with any degree of psychological determinism. The view to which Locke at times seemed to be working, which would hold a man free so far as his actions were moral or the expression of his 'true self' (and not of passing desires) was, as we have noted. held by Kant and recurs in Hegel and Bradley. Locke's difficulty over punishment – how can a man be justly punished if his action was necessitated? – has been recognised, by recent writers, following J. S. Mill and adopting a wholehearted reformatory (and not retributive) theory of punishment. (A reformatory theory is itself naturally deterministic.)

69

Part Two
Logic and Language

9 Ideas

(i) The Nature of Ideas

Locke defined 'idea' as 'whatsoever is the object of the under-standing when a man thinks'.[1] Ideas are the entities of which words are the signs. They are (in a sense to be considered below) 'in the mind'. But Locke never clears up the obvious problems which arise from these statements.

It would have helped if he had distinguished clearly between the mental acts of 'thinking' (perceiving, imagining etc.) and the ideas with which these acts are concerned. The mental acts are 'in the mind' in the sense that they are states of mind. 'It is certain that there is some alteration in my mind when I think of a figure which I did not think of before.'[2] But the idea itself (the figure or colour) cannot be 'in the mind' in the same sense.

Imagining provides the best illustration of this issue. We normally suppose that, when we are asked to imagine a dog, we have an *image* of a dog. It would make sense if we were asked: 'What kind of dog have you imagined? What is its colour?' Now the activity of imagining is certainly 'in the mind', but what about the image? We assume it depends on the mind. It is created by the activity of imagining and ceases to exist the moment that activity ceases. So too with Locke's ideas. The activities of perceiving, thinking, imagining and remembering are all 'in the mind'. The ideas entertained during these activities are dependent on the mind. They cease to exist the moment the activity ceases. Unfortunately Locke does not stick to this distinction between act and object clearly. In the passage from which the previous quotation is taken, the two are confused: 'I desire to be informed how my mind knows that the thinking on, *or the idea of the figure*, is not a modification of the mind.'[3] [My italics.]

D

73

But, if the distinction is retained, what is the status and nature of ideas? In further reflections on Malebranche, Locke says: 'Ideas may be real beings, though not substances, as motion is a real being though not a substance.'[4] But he also attacks Malebranche for saying that an idea 'is not a substance' but is 'a spiritual thing'. 'This spiritual thing, therefore, must either be a spiritual substance, or a mode of spirtiual substance, or a relation, for besides these I have no conception of anything.'[5] What then of Locke's ideas which are 'in the mind'? Are they minds or modes of minds or relations? Locke gives reasons why they cannot be 'in the mind' in any literal sense.

The mind or soul that perceives is one immaterial indivisible substance. Now I see the black and white on this paper. I hear one singing in the next room, I feel the warmth of the fire I sit by, and I taste an apple I am eating, and all this at the same time. Now I ask, take 'modification' for what you please, can the same unextended indivisible substance have different nay inconsistent (as these of black and white must be) modifications at the same time? Or must we suppose distinct parts in an indivisible substance, one for black, another for white, and another for red ideas?[6]

Locke thinks that ideas literally include the qualities apprehended such as colour and shape. And it can be asked how a state of mind can have a colour and a shape.

There is a general problem about Locke's theory of ideas. Why does he suppose that all kinds of mental activity involved the 'having of ideas', that is the apprehension of entities which are not substances and are dependent on the mind for their existence? There seem to be two factors explaining this. One is the assimilation of 'idea' to 'image', which is reinforced by the special experiences of perception and memory. For in these cases, as will be argued below, it is plausible to maintain that there is an entity (sense-datum or memory image) which literally *has* the characteristics of shape, colour etc., which we apprehend, though its existence depends on the mind. This is then extended to other mental activities such as reasoning, deliberating, pretending, predicting, where it is by no means so plausible to maintain that these involve the apprehension of mind-dependent entities. This tendency is reinforced by the description of an idea as what is

74

meant by a word. To understand a sentence requires the understanding of its constituent words. And the meaning of a word is taken to be an idea. This belief comes up against a host of difficulties.

The number of words used to express the meaning of a sentence varies from language to language and may vary within a given language. Understanding a sentence need not involve apprehending something called 'the meaning' of the sentence. It may involve being ready to respond in certain ways, knowing how to act, behaving intelligently, and a great variety of other possibilities.

Nevertheless there remain two examples where it is plausible to speak of 'having an idea' in the sense of being aware of a particular datum; these are the examples of memory and perception.

The latter example is particularly important to Locke in view of his empiricist programme, which attempts to trace to sensation and reflection (introspection) all the basic elements of experience. Here indeed are the seeds of the whole English empiricist tradition. If sensation is separated from all elements of memory, classification, objective reference, prediction, and other similar cognitive acts or attitudes, it is natural to hold that what sensation gives us is something of the same type as a mental image; for example, a round red patch, though the words 'red' and 'round' are inappropriate to describe it, as involving classification and abstraction.

This basic element is the 'sense-datum' of later epistemology, the element directly apprehended from which all experience is built up. The programmes of Moore, Russell, Broad and Price are all recognisably akin to the programme of Locke: to identify and describe the basic elements of experience, which are directly given and apprehended with certainty, and to examine the methods by which, from this basic material, knowledge of the world around us and the apprehension of such other truth (mathematical and philosophical) as we can attain may be derived. The main difference between these modern theories and Locke is that they pay little attention to ideas of reflection (or introspection).

This whole approach has been subjected to recent criticism originating mainly from Wittgenstein. The conception of the sense-datum has been widely discarded. An early example of this critical approach is G. A. Paul's article "Is There a Problem about Sense-Data"[7] and a full-length development of it is to be found in the work of J. L. Austin.[8]

The first example which we cited of an activity which is plausibly regarded as involving the apprehension of a datum similar in nature to a sense-datum was imagination, the creation of mental images. Even this has been effectively attacked by G. Ryle.[9] Certainly in a great many senses of the word 'imagine', mental images are absent or irrelevant. Ryle even doubts whether in such imagining as is properly called visualising the mind is seeing or contemplating a picture.

As to memory, the memory-image has also come under criticism. If there is an image at all, it may be an irrelevant extra in the experience, as when my childhood memory of going to the dentist is accompanied by a vivid picture of the dentist's moustache seen from below. Moreover, the whole interpretation of memory in terms of memory-images (as by Russell in *The Analysis of Mind*, chapter x) has been attacked, for example, by R. F. Holland.[10] And the very notion of a memory-image as an entity in its own right has come under fire. 'The mental image is not an entity but the way an object appears when it enters into a memory situation.'[11] This recalls the rejection of sense-data. When a mountain looks blue the sense-datum theory maintains that there is an entity (the sense-datum), which is other than the mountain, and really is blue. But the correct description of the situation is in terms of a multiple relation between the mind, the mountain, appearing and blue.

(ii) *Ideas and Propositions*

In ordinary language 'idea' is frequently equivalent to 'proposition', and an idea would be expressed not by a word but by a complete sentence. 'My ideas' on free trade or the Homeric problem are the propositions which I believe or am inclined to believe to be true or false on these topics. This is not acceptable in all uses because of the assimilation of 'idea' to 'image' in certain cases. My ideas concerning Lloyd George are that he was the founder of national health insurance, the leader of the nation in war, and the man who split the Liberal Party – and these are all propositions. But I also have an idea of Lloyd George as I saw him in 1920, the vivid picture of the white-maned cloaked figure, and this picture is not a proposition.

At Locke's time, the current philosophical tradition, springing from Descartes, found truth and certainty of knowledge in the apprehension of clear and distinct ideas. For Locke, however, the

76

unit for truth and falsehood is not the idea but the proposition. This is made clear in the *Essay* 'Truth and falsehood belong only to propositions. When ideas are termed true or false there is some tacit proposition involved.'[12] 'Ideas in themselves are neither true nor false.'[13] This view is further stressed in Locke's reply to Stillingfleet who had followed Descartes in making knowledge consist of the apprehension of clear and distinct ideas. 'Nor is it one idea by itself that, in this or any case, makes us certain; but certainty consists in the perceived agreement or disagreement of distinct ideas as they stand in the proposition whose truth or falsehood we would be certain of.'[14]

This insight of Locke's was generally accepted by later logicians and it had also the authority of Leibniz, for whom the proposition was the unit for logic. But it led to a development closely parallel to the sense-datum theory. As experience was there to be analysed into sense-data and the various operations performed with them, so in later logical developments all mental activities were to be analysed in terms of propositions and the various activities to be performed with them. Thus the proposition 'that the earth is flat' can be affirmed, denied, doubted, supposed as a premiss in inference, inferred from other premisses, etc. The parallel to the neutral 'having an idea' (without any concomitant logical activities) or 'sensing a sense-datum' would be 'entertaining a proposition'. Up to Russell and the Wittgenstein of the *Tractatus*, modern logic rested on this basis. Again doubts have arisen. Early specimens are the articles "What Does Mr. W. E. Johnson Mean by a Proposition?" by H. W. B. Joseph;[15] and "Are There Propositions?" by G. Ryle.[16] And again the influence of the later work of Wittgenstein has reinforced these criticisms. As ideas were the shadow correlates of words, so propositions (that x is y) like facts (that x is y) are the shadow correlates of sentences (as their 'structure' shows). An alternative analysis in terms of sentences and objects is needed.

(iii) *Innate Ideas*
Book I of the *Essay* is an attack on innate ideas. There has been much debate on the question against whom this attack was directed. On the continent, the theory of innate ideas was held by Descartes and his successors, with whose work Locke was certainly familiar. Descartes divided ideas into adventitious (ideas such as colour and heat, caused in the mind by external stimuli), factitious

(created by the mind itself, e.g. chimaera, centaur), and innate (arising from the mind's own inherent nature).

'Innate' could have two meanings. An innate idea could be found in all minds from the beginning of their existence (which for Descartes went back to the life of the foetus in the womb) and therefore in the minds of newly-born children. When it was objected to Descartes that the minds of children were not stocked with mathematical, metaphysical and theological ideas, he advanced the alternative theory that an innate idea is a capacity for having ideas. In some families we say certain diseases such as gout or gravel are innate 'not because the babes of these families suffer from these diseases in their mother's womb, but because they are born with a disposition or tendency to contract them.'[17] The disease is hereditary but environment has to provide the occasion for its occurrence. So with innate ideas. Indeed it might be possible for an idea to be innate in a man's mind and yet for it never to have actually presented itself to him through the whole of his conscious life.

But besides Descartes and his followers there were other thinkers whom Locke must have had in mind. J. W. Yolton[18] has shown, by a survey of contemporary English thought, that the theory of innate ideas was very widely held among English theologians in the seventeenth century in both the forms current among the Cartesians, namely the 'occurrent' and the 'potential' versions of the theory distinguished in the preceding paragraph.

Included in the knowledge held to be innate by both Cartesian and English schools of thought were the laws of thought, the basic principles of mathematics, the rules of morals, and of course, above all, the idea of God.

Locke's arguments against innate ideas fall into three groups. First he attacks the assumption on which the theory rests, the assumption that these ideas must be innate because they are universal and necessary. Because an idea is universal it need not be innate and in any case the ideas in question are not universally accepted.[19] The force of this argument depends on the alternative account Locke promises[20] and attempts to give in Book IV of the *Essay*, discussed in chapter 10 (pp. 81-6).

The second line of attack urges that children and idiots do not have such ideas.

The third goes on to consider the second or 'potential' version of the theory. Locke asks whether all men at all times have the *capacity* to entertain such ideas, and again idiots and children are cited as exceptions. When therefore does the capacity emerge? The stock answer was 'when men come to the use of reason'. This may mean one of two things, either that reason itself discovers these ideas or that the awakening of reason and the capacity to be aware of them is simultaneous. The first alternative is dismissed because reason is limited to demonstration, that is, to the apprehension that something follows from something else. But these ideas are not supposed to depend on others, but to be self-evident. As for simultaneous awakening, this also will not do. Children can reason long before they can apprehend such ideas as impossibility or identity.[21]

Locke's full solution of the problem of necessary and self-evident truth appears in Book IV where he has to reconcile it with his principle that all our ideas arise from sensation and introspection. But in the course of his polemic against innate ideas a solution is foreshadowed. It rests on the distinction between ideas and propositions noted in the preceding section. It is noticeable that Locke's attack is headed "No Innate Principles in the Mind", and almost all the examples given are examples not of ideas but of propositions. Similarly, the following chapter is headed "No Innate Practical Principles", and the examples are moral laws.

Locke points out that, as soon as sweetness and bitterness are experienced, it is self-evident that they differ, and similarly that a rod is not a cherry. In fact, all propositions asserting difference are self-evidently and necessarily true and therefore all should be innate. But 'since no proposition can be innate unless the ideas about which it be innate, this will be to suppose all our ideas of colours, sounds, tastes, figure etc., innate, than which there cannot be anything more opposite to reason and experience'.[22] Locke here suggests that ideas may be adventitious or derived from experience yet some of the relations between them may be self-evident and necessary. There are, however, some places where Locke refers to ideas, not principles, as innate (God, impossibility, identity) and it might seem that the solution suggested would not apply to them. Locke's views on moral truth are discussed in chapter 12.

The rejection of innate ideas in Locke's *Essay* was a principal reason for the very critical reception it was accorded.[23] For many theologians, usually horrified by doctrines such as those of Hobbes, the notion of religious and moral truth imprinted on the heart of

79

man was a basic and essential belief. The alternatives they foresaw were atheism, scepticism and moral relativism. The doctrine of innate ideas continued to have distinguished adherents – notably Leibniz. But there has been no trace of it in recent thought. The problems with which it was devised to deal recur as the questions whether all ideas are derived from experience; whether any truths are self-evident and necessary, and, if so, how they are apprehended, and in particular what is the epistemological status of mathematical, moral and theological propositions.

AB p 131

10 Knowledge

Knowledge is defined by Locke as 'the perception of agreement or disagreement of two ideas'.[1] There are four sorts of agreement: identity (or diversity); relation; coexistence or necessary connection; and real existence.[2] Of these four, the standard case of knowledge is the second. Knowledge of identity and diversity (white is white, white is not red) is 'trifling'. Knowledge of coexistence (by which Locke means the coexistence of qualities in an object) is unattainable. Knowledge of real existence is very limited, and also dubiously described as knowledge of an agreement between two ideas. With these latter categories we shall be concerned later.

(i) Knowledge of Relations between Ideas

The prime example of 'knowledge of relations' is mathematics. It is unfortunate that Locke defines his third sort of knowledge as 'coexistence or necessary connection' for it is primarily in mathematics that 'agreement' means necessary connection or implication (and 'disagreement' means incompatibility).

Provided that our mathematical ideas are clear and distinct, we are able to apprehend necessary connections between them, either directly or through intermediate steps.[3] Locke insists that mathematical knowledge is throughout hypothetical. Mathematical ideas are the creation of the mind, and their connection with each other is wholly independent of the existence in the real world of any object which corresponds with them. 'The mathematician considers the truth and properties belonging to a

D*

rectangle or circle only as they are ideas in his own mind. For it is possible he never found either of them existing mathematically, i.e. precisely true, in his life.'[4] 'All the discourses of the mathematicians about the squaring of a circle, conic sections, or any other part of mathematics concern not the existence of any of those figures; but their demonstrations which depend on their ideas are the same whether there be any square or circle existing in the world or no.'[5] Plato had been the first to recognise this feature of mathematical argument and regarded it as a weakness in its nature. A so-called mathematical proof of proposition c shows only that it follows necessarily from proposition b which itself follows from proposition a. If they are true, it is true. Plato thought that the truth of the basic propositions of mathematics must depend on truths established outside mathematics, and ultimately on one final truth. Aristotle, on the other hand, thought that the basic propositions of mathematics were peculiar to mathematics and that their truth could be intuitively apprehended.

The basic propositions of mathematics are definitions and axioms. Locke's view that mathematical ideas are created by the mind of the mathematician is essentially the modern view that definitions are arbitrary and not true or false. It is therefore only in the case of the axioms that it is plausible to maintain that they are intuitively certain or self-evident. Locke does not deny their certainty; what he does deny very effectively is that they are among the basic premises from which mathematical truths follow.

These 'principles' (things equal to the same thing are equal to each other; the whole is equal to the sum of its parts) are both insufficient and unnecessary as the premises of mathematical reasoning: insufficient because 'a man may pore long enough on these maxims without ever seeing one jot the more of mathematical truth'; unnecessary because 'the mind had other objects, other views before it, far different from those maxims, when it first got the knowledge of such truths in mathematics, which men well acquainted enough with those received axioms, but ignorant of their method who first made these demonstrations, can never sufficiently admire.'[6]

The belief that the axiom 'things equal to the same thing are equal to each other' is a necessary premiss in mathematical reasoning is due to the belief that reasoning must be syllogistic, and that, from particular premises without general principles, no

82

(see p. 117)

conclusion follows. With the axiom as major premiss, and 'A and c are equal to the same thing B' as the minor premiss, it can be validly concluded that A equals c. The claim that this formulation is required for a valid conclusion, and that the inference A = B, B = C, therefore A = C is invalid without the axiom, can be refuted by the recognition that the axiom is not a premiss in inference but the principle of inference. In syllogistic argument a similar principle (the *dictum de omni et nullo*) can be formulated, and it would then be arguable that no syllogism is valid without the *dictum* as a major premiss. Locke's account of the status of such principles is dealt with below (pp. 85-6).

The other field in which Locke thought that necessary connections between ideas could be directly apprehended is that of morals. As in mathematics, moral concepts are created by the mind. They can therefore be clearly defined. Their connections with each other are, as in mathematics, hypothetical. They are independent of the real existence of examples of their terms. Locke became progressively more doubtful about this claim. The evidence for this, along with the examples he gives of moral truths thus apprehended, is considered in chapter 12 (pp. 116-18).

Both in mathematics and in morals, Locke would appear to be a rationalist. The element of empiricism which survives in these fields is that, although moral and mathematical ideas are the work of the individual mind and have no necessary counterparts in reality, the materials of which these ideas are composed are derived ultimately from sensation or introspection. In the case of morals this derivation is reasonably straightforward, except in one respect. Ideas such as law, obedience, theft, killing, seem as easily analysable into constituents ultimately given in experience as any other complex ideas. The special difficulty is the specifically moral term (good, bad, right, wrong) or the concealed moral element in a complex idea (such as murder, property). For the former, the only solution available is the hedonistic solution. 'Things are good or evil only in reference to pleasure or pain. . . . Pleasure and pain and that which causes them, good and evil, are the hinges on which our passions turn.'[7] For the latter the same answer might be given. Alternatively 'murder' and 'property' might be defined as 'unlawful killing' and 'lawful possession' and the empirical source would then be legal facts. But this solution would mean that the 'necessary truths' in question would no longer be moral truths and would be empirical and not *a priori*.

83

In regard to mathematics, empirical derivation of its ideas is not so easy. We have seen that all ideas of number are supposed by Locke to be derived from the simple idea of unity (which is given with every datum of sense or introspection) along with the operations of addition and subtraction (chapter 1, p. 19.) Arithmetic being thus accounted for, we have next to deal with geometry. Space is a simple idea.[8] But it is very difficult to pin down exactly what Locke means here by 'space'. It does not seem possible that Locke thought, as Kant did, that infinite space can be given in intuition. Yet he says that every different distance or different space is a simple mode of this idea.[9] Figures too are modes of the simple idea of space. In what sense then is space given in perception as a simple idea? Not in the sense of 'position' or 'place' as Locke calls it, for this is a relational idea involving the relations between one object and others. The answer which seems to come nearest to Locke's intentions is extendedness. An idea of sight includes, besides its colour, the idea of extension. From this by multiplication and division we can achieve the ideas of infinity, of lines and points, and we can then build up all the spatial ideas necessary for geometry.[10]

Here then is the basic link between mathematical thinking and experience which differentiates Locke from pure rationalists like Descartes for whom the basic ideas of mathematics as well as the truth of its demonstrations were independent of experience.

But this in turn means that there is a further and most vital link with experience. Mathematical (like moral) thinking is not a wholly intellectual game bearing no relation to reality. The thinking is hypothetical and hypothetical about the real world.

> The knowledge we have of mathematical truths is not only certain but real knowledge and not the bare empty vision of vain insignificant chimeras of the brain. . . . The mathematician considers the truth and properties belonging to a rectangle or circle only as they are ideas in his own mind. For it is possible he never found either of them existing mathematically, i.e. precisely true, in his life. But yet the knowledge he has of any truths or properties belonging to a circle or any other mathematical figure are nevertheless certain and true even of real things existing; because real things are no further concerned nor intended to be meant by any such propositions, than as things really agree to those archetypes in his mind.[11]

84

This also is his reply to Stillingfleet, who objects to the parallel between mathematical and theological argument drawn by Locke because 'those ideas, on which mathematical demonstrations proceed, are wholly in the mind and do not relate to the existence of things'. Locke replies that mathematical reasoning 'takes in all those things, really existing, which answer to those ideas'.[12] Applied mathematics, as 'the incomparable Newton' had shown, is the basis of scientific advance. Locke points out to Stillingfleet that the points made about mathematics are equally valid and important concerning moral theory. Moral ideas, though entirely mind-dependent in their complex structure, owe their materials to experience, and the truth of their demonstrations is applicable to experience, wherever an object or event in reality corresponds to the definitions of the ideas involved, such as theft or murder.

Indeed just as the derivation of moral ideas from experience is easier than that of mathematical ideas so their application to reality is easier also. That an event was a theft seems to be more easily ascertainable with accuracy and finality than that a certain line in the world is straight or a certain track circular.

(ii) Logical and Mathematical Axioms

We have seen that Locke denied that mathematical axioms were necessary as premises for the truth of any mathematical conclusion. He deals with these and with self-evident logical axioms (the Principles of Identity and Difference) in his chapter on 'Maxims'.[13]

He argues that the self-evidence which is claimed for these axioms is not restricted to them but characterises also particular propositions. 'A thing is what it is and differs from any other thing' is no more or less self-evident than 'white is white and not red'. Moreover we come to know the particular propositions first and without any reference to or need for the axioms. Axioms then are of no use to prove or confirm less general propositions; they are not the foundations of any scientific knowledge; they are no help in scientific discovery. They have a double use. They can help in teaching a science, in cases where a pupil cannot see the necessary connection in the particular case, but may see it as an application of the axiom. They can also help in resolving disputes. The disputant cannot reject the axiom and then has only to be shown that the particular issue exemplifies it. An example of the latter use is G. E. Moore's *Principia Ethica*, which takes as its text 'everything is what it is and not another thing' and then argues that particular terms (e.g. 'good' and 'pleasant') which have been identified with each other require to be distinguished.

The logical status of axioms is not entirely clear in Locke. In 1664 in the third *Essay on the Law of Nature* held he that 'the first and best-known principle of the sciences (namely that it is impossible that the same thing at the same time should both be and not be) . . . is not inscribed by nature as an axiom in our hearts nor taken for granted by anyone before he has either learned it from another or (which is the proper method of establishing principles) proved it to himself by induction and by observing particulars.'[14]

This view, that the basic logical axioms or 'Laws of Thought' are established by induction from particulars (i.e. from particular instances, such as 'white is white' 'white is not red'), does not appear in the *Essay Concerning Human Understanding*. In arguing there that the axiom is not required as a premiss for a piece of mathematical reasoning or for the apprehension of particular identities and differences, he maintains that the piece of mathematical reasoning or the apprehension that white is not red is as self-evident as the axiom. This would imply that the axioms are self-evident. In what sense then if any does the apprehension of their necessary truth require the previous apprehension of particular pieces of argument or particular necessary connections? Locke's answer seems to be 'not at all', except in the purely temporal sense that particular ideas precede general ideas. A child knows that three and four equal seven 'as soon as he has settled in his mind the clear and distinct ideas that these names stand for; and then he knows the truth of that proposition upon the same grounds and by the same means as he knew before that a rod and a cherry are not the same thing; and upon the same ground also that he may come to know afterwards that it is impossible for the same thing to be and not to be.'[15]

The argument implied is that, as soon as the terms in the axiom are clearly understood, the truth of the axiom is self-evident; but the terms of axioms are among the most abstract and general ideas possible, and therefore appear very late in the development of the human mind; and therefore the apprehension of the self-evidence of the axioms is a late achievement too.

(An interesting illustration of Locke's claim comes from the Greek language. Greek colour words tend to be fairly specific. There is no word for 'blue' to cover the range from deep to light blue and from the purple border to the green border. Nor, until late, is there a word for 'colour' – for the family including blue, red, green etc. The word which later meant 'colour' at first meant 'skin-complexion'. But what about the family resemblance between blueness, cleverness, roundness and immortality? There is no word for what all those have in common – that they are all *qualities* – until Plato coined the word in one of his later dialogues.)

(iii) Knowledge of Coexistence

Locke points out that we experience ideas grouped together and can therefore enquire whether these grouped ideas have any necessary connection with each other. This applies particularly to our ideas of species of substances which are 'nothing but collections of simple ideas united in one subject and so coexisting together'.[16] But enquiry reveals few necessary connections here. 'The simple ideas whereof our complex ideas of substances are made up are, for the most part, such as carry with them, in their own nature, no visible necessary connection or inconsistency with any other simple ideas whose coexistence with them we would inform ourselves about.'[17] Locke thinks this is due to our ignorance of the relation between our ideas of secondary qualities and the primary qualities (vibrations etc.) in objects which cause them. The implication that if we could discover the primary qualities of objects we could apprehend necessary connections between them is discussed below (p. 94). But even without that there is a weakness. It is not only between the secondary qualities of objects that we fail to see any necessary connection. There is no such seen connection between the shape and the size, or the motion and the weight of a piece of gold. So we have to rely solely on experience for these connections also.

> Of all the qualities that are coexistent in any subject, without this dependence and evident connection of their ideas one with another, we cannot know certainly any two to coexist any further than experience by our senses informs us. Thus though we see the yellow colour, and upon trial, find the weight, malleableness, fusibility and fixedness that are united in a piece of gold: yet because no one of these ideas has any evident dependence or necessary connection with the other we cannot certainly know that, where any four of these are, the fifth will be there also, however highly probable soever it be; because the

highest probability amounts not to certainty, without which there can be no true knowledge.[18]

Locke thinks there are a few cases where we can apprehend a necessary connection between primary qualities. 'Figure necessarily supposes extension; receiving or communicating motion by impulse supposes solidity.' But this is not limited to primary qualities; colour supposes extension. And in any case these connections are general; they do not explain the connection between the shape and size of a nugget.

Knowledge of incompatibility goes further than that of necessary coexistence. Each specific quality excludes other qualities of the same species.[19] But again this is general, and does not explain the incompatibilities in which we tend to believe (blue nuggets or black swans).

If the belief in the coexistence of qualities we show in our expectations about substances falls short of knowledge, so *a fortiori* do our beliefs about causes. 'As to the powers of substances to change the sensible qualities of other bodies which make a great parts of our enquiries about them and is no inconsiderable branch of our knowledge I doubt as to these whether our knowledge reaches much farther than our experience.'[26]

At this point a comparison with Hume will bring out the peculiarities of Locke's position. A number of questions naturally occur. Why is it highly probable that experienced groupings or causal connections will recur? Is this not merely, as Hume thought, a belief due to the association of ideas? The more often a sequence occurs the more we expect it to recur. But is not this belief wholly irrational? Locke regarded the association of ideas as 'something unreasonable in man'.[21] But he goes on to say

Some of our ideas have a natural correspondence and connection one with another; it is the office and excellency of our reason to trace these and hold them together in that union and correspondence which is founded in their peculiar beings. Besides this there is another connection of ideas wholly owing to chance or custom; ideas that in themselves are not all of kin come to be so united in some men's minds that it is very hard to separate them; they always keep in company and the one no sooner comes into the understanding but its associate appears with it.[22]

The difficulty is obvious. The qualities that go to make up a substance, and the effects that 'follow from' causes, have no 'natural correspondence with each other' and are not 'all of kin'. Why then are our beliefs in their coherence not due to the association of ideas, that 'disease of the mind. which is 'so frequent a cause of error and mistake'?[23] The remedy for the disease is

> to take heed . . . that . . . ideas that have no natural cohesion come not to be united in their heads . . . that they never suffer any ideas to be joined in their understandings in any other or stronger combination than what their own nature and correspondence give them, and that they often examine those that they find linked together in their minds whether this association of ideas be from the visible agreement that is in the ideas themselves or from the habitual and prevailing custom of the mind joining them thus together in thinking.[24]

No third choice is offered, and the way lies open to Hume. There seem to be three factors which saved Locke from this conclusion. First, as we have seen, he thought (though without any adequate grounds) that some existential necessary connections (between primary quality ideas) and some existential incompatibilities (between ideas belonging to different species of the same genus) were knowable. Secondly, he thought (as we shall see below), but again without adequate grounds, that if we could discover the minute constitution of bodies we should know their interactions as necessary connections. Since our ideas depend on these microscopic interactions they too are necessarily connected, even if we cannot know in detail what the connections are. Thirdly, Locke differed from Hume in maintaining that the general principles of co-inherence in a substance and of causal efficacy were known to be true with rational necessity. The red colour of a cherry necessarily presupposes a substance in which to inhere and therefore a necessary connection with the other qualities of that substance whatever they may be (see chapter 3, p. 30). He also claimed to know with certainty that every event has a cause, and therefore that there is a necessary connection between the falling of this apple and some event or other which is its cause (see chapter 4, p. 39). Granted these two certainties (which Hume denied), it becomes proper to look for other regularly coexistent qualities or other regularly preceding events, and to regard their connection with the quality or event in question as probable in proportion to the regularity of the conjunction.

It must be admitted that Locke does not seem to have realised the dilemma into which he had put himself by his late recognition of the association of ideas. Nor therefore does the Kantian type of solution which we have proposed for him appear in his works.

It is to be noted that all the connections and exclusions established by experience concern only our own ideas and not the real world. They relate, in Locke's language, nominal essences, not real essences. They predict experiences, not objects or events. We enquire what qualities or powers substances have or have not 'which is nothing else but to know what other simple ideas do or do not co-exist with those that make up that complex idea'.[25] This naturally leads us to ask whether and how far Locke claimed knowledge going beyond his own ideas.

(iv) Knowledge of Real Existence

Locke's description of 'idea' as 'whatsoever is the object of the understanding when a man thinks' presented him with the difficulty of justifying any knowledge or belief concerning the existence of objects corresponding to these ideas.

The difficulty is basically a *logical* difficulty. For example Locke held that our ideas of primary qualities correspond to real primary qualities in bodies. But in the interpretation of this sentence, 'real primary qualities in bodies' are objects of the understanding when a man thinks. Therefore they are ideas.

Locke admits the difficulty. 'Our knowledge, therefore, is real only so far as there is a conformity between our ideas and the reality of things. But what shall be here the criterion? How shall the mind when it perceives nothing but its own ideas know that they agree with things themselves'?[26] 'How can I know the picture of anything is like that thing, when I never see that which it represents.'[27] And it was repeatedly urged against him by Stillingfleet. 'Reason cannot perceive the connection between the objects and the ideas.'[28] As we shall see, Locke thinks we can know there are real objects because we know that something must cause our simple ideas of sensation. But the logical difficulty comes out when he says that this belief concerns the agreement of two ideas (and not the relation between an idea and a real world).

90

The two ideas that in this case are perceived to agree, and do thereby produce knowledge, are the idea of actual sensation (which is an action whereof I have a clear and distinct idea) and the idea of actual existence of something without me that causes that sensation. And what other certainty your lordship has by your senses of the existing of anything without you, but the perceived connection of those two ideas, I would gladly know.[29]

The only exit from this logical difficulty would be for Locke to admit that, in some cases, there can be direct knowledge of real objects, without the mediation of ideas. The repesentative theory of ideas might then become, for example, a representative theory of perception (but not of all thought).

When Locke comes on to ask in detail which are the cases in which we have knowledge of real existence, he answers: 'We have knowledge of our own existence by intuition; of the existence of God by demonstration; and of other things by sensation.'[30]

It has been argued above (chapter 6, p. 56) that the representative theory of ideas breaks down over knowledge of the existence of my self. I am directly aware of pain itself (and not merely of an idea of it). And the logical necessity of a subject to support an attribute makes me certain of the existence of the subject of the pain—myself.[31] This certainty does not extend to the past and future existence of my self.

The demonstration of the existence of God is considered in chapter 13 (pp. 129–31); and it therefore remains to examine our knowledge of the existence 'of other things by sensation'. There is a 'manifest difference' between my idea of the sun when I look on it by day and when I think on it by night.[32] And one difference is that the former idea forces itself upon me and I cannot avoid having it. Hence I can argue that the idea is caused in my mind by an external object. 'Therefore it must needs be some exterior cause and the brisk acting of some objects without me whose efficacy I cannot resist that produces those ideas in my mind, whether I will or no.'[33]

Locke is aware that there is a strong argument against this conclusion, arising from dreams and hallucinations. Both of them (or at any rate the nightmare kind of dream and the mirage kind of hallucination) have the 'tang of reality' and the characteristic of forcing themselves upon us whether we will or no. He makes two separate replies to this: first that there is a great difference between being in a fire and dreaming one is in it, especially the pain caused by the former. But this reply fails because there is dream pain and fear. The second reply is that if there is no distinction between dream and reality, then he who questions whether we dream may himself be dreaming and so 'it is not much matter that a waking man should answer him'.[34]

The other question is this. Admitting the causal argument, why should we suppose our ideas of sensation are caused by material objects or 'bodies'? Berkeley, using the same argument, concluded that they were caused by God. On this, Locke has simply the strong conviction of the ordinary man. And it is perhaps some feeling of the weakness here that makes him admit that the certainty of the existence of material things falls short of knowledge. 'This notice we have by our senses of the existing of things without us, though it be not altogether so certain as our intuitive knowledge or the deductions of our reason employed about the clear abstract ideas of our own minds; yet it is an assurance that deserves the name of knowledge.'[35]

What then may we say in detail about the material objects which cause our sensations? We have seen that Locke believed that they have the primary qualities (shape, size, motion, solidity) but not necessarily qualities exactly similar to the ideas of primary qualities we apprehend in sensation. Locke says we know about the constitution of bodies only that they have the powers to cause in us the ideas of sensation. 'We do not see that internal constitution from whence these powers flow.' But 'that is a good argument to show how short our philosophical speculations are about the real internal constitutions of things.'[36]

By 'philosophical speculations' Locke here means 'scientific hypotheses' ('natural philosophy'=science). Of such hypotheses Locke regarded the corpuscular hypothesis as the most convincing available. 'The modern corpuscularians talk in most things more intelligibly than the peripatetics, who possessed the schools immediately before them.'[37] The corpuscularian hypothesis is 'that which is thought to go furthest in an intelligible explanation of those qualities of bodies; and I fear the weakness of human understanding is scarce able to substitute another which will afford us a fuller and clearer discovery of the necessary connection and co-existence of the powers which are to be observed united in several sorts of them.'[38]

But it remains a hypothesis and therefore lacking in certainty. *A fortiori* any particular hypothesis, e.g. about the minute structure of gold, must be even further from certainty. There is thus no science of bodies ('science' in Locke's sense involving knowledge and being typified by mathematics). 'Therefore am I apt to doubt that how far soever human industry may advance useful and experimental philosophy in physical things, scientifical will still be out of our reach. . . . Certainty and demonstration are things we must not in these matters pretend to.'[39] 'Inquisitive and observing men may by strength of judgement penetrate further and, on probabilities taken from wary observation, and hints well laid together, often guess right at what experience has not yet discovered to them. But this is guessing still; it amounts only to opinion and has not that certainty which is requisite to knowledge.'[40]

Among such specific hypotheses is that concerning the way in which ideas of colour and visual shape are produced in the mind. Light consists of particles reflected from a body with a type of motion suited to produce the sensation, for example, of white in us. These particles may be globules and their motion a rotation, but in the *Essay* Locke does not commit himself to details.[41]

The most detailed expression of his views on this topic occurs in connection with Malebranche.

I think the perception we have of bodies at a distance from us may be accounted for, so far as we are capable of understanding it, by the motion of particles coming from them and striking on our organs. In feeling and tasting, there is immediate contact. Sound is not unintelligibly explained by a vibrating motion communicated to the medium, and the effluvia of odorous bodies will, without any great difficulty, account for smells. . . . He that shall allow extreme smallness in the particles of light and exceeding swiftness in their motion . . . and that, of a million of rays that rebound from any visible area of the body, perhaps the thousandth or ten thousandth part coming to the eye are enough to move the retina sufficiently to cause a sensation in the mind, will not find any great difficulty.[42]

Locke goes on to point out that a number of objects may be seen simultaneously because the retina is extended in area and therefore capable of recording a picture representing a complex visual scene. But he remains well aware that the transition between a picture on the retina and an idea in the mind is not explained by this scientific story. 'Impressions made on the retina by rays of light I think I understand; and motions from thence continued to the brain may be conceived, and that these produce ideas in our minds I am persuaded, but in a manner to me incomprehensible.'[43]

The recognition by Locke of the distinction between demonstration and the probability which attaches to scientific theories is perhaps the best example of his main achievement, which is the mapping of the intellectual world and the insistence that methods of thinking and criteria of truth must vary with the subject-matter of each type of enquiry.

Locke himself, however, did not have a firm grip on this vital distinction. For he connects the failure of physical hypotheses to attain certainty with our lack of clear ideas concerning the primary qualities of the minute constituents of bodies 'without which we cannot tell what effects they will produce.'[44]

> If we could discover the figure, size, texture and motion of the minute constituent parts of any two bodies, we should know without trial several of their operations one upon another as we do now the properties of a square or a triangle. . . . Did we know the mechanical affections of the particles of rhubarb, hemlock, opium, and a man, as a watchmaker does those of a watch, whereby it performs its operations, and of a file, which by rubbing on them will alter the figure of any of the wheels, we should be able to tell beforehand that rhubarb will purge, hemlock kill and opium make a man sleep; as well as a watchmaker can that a little piece of paper laid on the balance will keep a watch from going until it be removed; or that, some small part of it being rubbed by a file, the machine would quite lose its motion and the watch go no more. . . . But while we are destitute of senses acute enough to discover the minute particles of bodies and to give us ideas of their mechanical affections, we must be content to be ignorant of their properties and ways of operation.[45]

Locke is here maintaining that if we had microscopes capable of revealing the atomic constituents of matter, the empirical and experimental elements in science would disappear, and its con-

94

clusions would have not merely high probability but the demonstrative certainty characteristic of mathematics. The example of the watchmaker is obviously misleading. The effects of weights on balance wheels or files on metal were not established without observation and experiment. Locke also overlooks here a point he makes elsewhere with great effect, that 'we are wont to consider the substances we meet with each of them as an entire thing in itself, having all its qualities in itself and independent of other things'; whereas the weight of gold, the fluidity of water, the pull of a magnet, the life and death of a plant or an animal are all due to relations with the rest of the world. For a complete explanation of anything we ought perhaps 'to look not only beyond this our earth and atmosphere but even beyond the sun and remotest star our eyes have yet discovered.'[46] So we should have to know the minute constitution of the universe in order to have certain knowledge of necessary connections between physical substances or events, and to make natural philosophy a science.

We return, however, to Locke's insistence that, in our present state, the study of nature must be pursued by experiment and observation and can result only in probable hypotheses. 'Experience here must teach me what reason cannot; and it is by trying alone that I can certainly know what other qualities coexist with those of my complex idea, e.g. whether that yellow, heavy, fusible body I call gold be malleable or no.'[47] We should not take up any hypothesis too hastily 'till we have very well examined particulars and made several experiments in that thing which we would explain by our hypothesis'.[48]

Locke draws three conclusions from this view of our study of nature.

First, the value of such study is its practical utility – it may be of greater value to mankind than 'works of charity'. The discovery of quinine or printing or the compass did more good than hospitals and almshouses. We may recall the passage where he reminds us that, from a practical point of view, it is just as well that we see a difference between red and green as colours rather than as (what they probably are) different motions in the particles of light (see chapter 2, p. 24).

Secondly, the fact that our conclusions are only probable hypotheses should lead to charity, forbearance and tolerance. 'It would become all men to maintain peace and the common offices of humanity and friendship in the diversity of opinions' . . . 'we

95

should do well to commiserate our mutual ignorance and endeavour to remove it in all the gentle and fair ways of information.'
It is also noticeable that the few men who have really examined
and tested their own scientific hypotheses – the great scientists –
'find so little reason to be magisterial in their opinions that
nothing insolent and imperious is to be expected from them'.[49]
The third conclusion is this.

God has set some things in broad daylight; as he has given us
certain knowledge, though limited to a few things . . . so, in the
greatest part of our concerns, he has afforded us only the twi-
light, as I may so say, of probability; . . . wherein, to check our
over-confidence and presumption, we might, by every day's
experience, be made sensible of our shortsightedness and liable-
ness to error; the sense whereof might be a constant admoni-
tion to us, to spend the days of this our pilgrimage with industry and care, in the search and following of that way which
might lead us to a state of greater perfection.[50]

Our proper employment lies in those enquiries, and in that sort
of knowledge which is most suited to our natural capacities, and
carries in it our greatest interest, i.e. the condition of our eternal
estate. Hence I think I may conclude, that morality is the
proper science and business of mankind in general, (who are
both concerned and fitted to search out their *summum bonum*).[51]

11 Language as a Source of Error

Locke regarded the imperfections and the abuse of language as sources of many fruitless disputes and philosophical errors. Words are the signs of ideas and their value lies first in recording our own ideas for future reference and second (and much more important) in communicating our ideas to others.

The words for simple ideas (white, yellow, sweet, bitter) give rise to fewest problems, first because only a single idea is concerned and second because the terms carry an obvious meaning.

The problems concerning a word which purports to stand for a complex idea are:

(a) that it may have no meaning at all;
(b) that its meaning may be obscure or confused;
(c) that it may not mean the same to one person as to another;
(d) that it may change its meaning in the course of an argument or in the course of time;
(e) that it may be misapplied;
(f) that it may lead to the assumption that there is some entity to which it refers, when its meaning may be otherwise explained.

In the case of simple ideas, the idea normally precedes the learning of the name. We see white, we taste bitter, we feel pain before we learn what to call these ideas. But with complex ideas the name often comes first, because the idea is not given in experience in the same direct way. It is true of course that 'in the beginning of language it was necessary to have the idea before one gave it the name, and so is still, where, making a new complex idea, one also by giving it a new name makes a new word'.[1]

Locke is not at all clear in distinguishing the six problems (*a*) to (*f*) listed above; and the examples he gives are not always easy to allocate to one head or another. Words must be without meaning to children before they have found out how to apply them. This applies especially to moral words – indeed 'these moral words are in most men's mouths little more than bare sounds'.[2] Another example of a meaningless word is one whose definition is self-contradictory.[3]

Moral ideas are mixed modes and are therefore mind-made, and this explains their liability to confusion. When they have any meaning 'it is for the most part but a very loose and undetermined and consequently obscure and confused signification'.[4] Examples are honour, faith, grace. As we have seen earlier, substance is another example. 'Of substance, we have no idea of what it is, but only a confused obscure one of what it does.'[5] To say that a man has an obscure idea is presumably to say that he cannot state clearly what his words mean. (It is interesting that this would be an example of Locke's sixth problem. Because he cannot say what he means, Locke assumes that he has an idea before his mind and that this idea has the characteristic of being obscure.) To say an idea is confused need not mean that a man has an idea and that it has the characteristic of being confused. It should mean that a man confuses two distinct ideas, either asserting that they are identical or using one when the other is appropriate. An example of the first, given on more than one occasion by Locke, is the Cartesian mistake of confusing body with extension. 'That body and extension in common use stand for two distinct ideas is plain to anyone that will but reflect a little . . . and yet there are those who find it necessary to confound their signification.'[6] The second is illustrated by the confusion of frugality with covetousness.[7]

The difficulties that a word may not mean the same to one person as to another and that it may change its meaning during an argument or with the passage of time are again obvious with mixed modes (and especially with moral ideas), for these are made by the individual mind; hence 'men's names of very compound ideas, such as for the most part are moral words, have seldom in two different men the same precise signification; since one man's complex idea seldom agrees with another's, and often differs from his own – from that which he had yesterday or will have tomorrow'.[8] But the problems are not limited to mixed modes. As we have seen, our ideas of particular kinds of substances (abstract general ideas) are also, for Locke, mind-dependent (see chapter 5, p. 46). One reason for this is that 'the simple ideas that coexist and are united in the same subject are very numerous' – indeed 'almost infinite' when one includes all the powers which a substance has. From this number each man makes his own selection and alters it at will. 'In the substance of gold, one satisfies himself with colour and weight, yet another thinks solubility in aqua regia as necessary to be joined with that colour in his idea of gold, as anyone else does its fusibility.'[9]

An example of misapplication of a word comes in the same context, for many people think that their idea of gold is its real essence when this real essence is unknowable. And what is called a confusion between frugality and covetousness may equally well be called a misapplication of terms.

Philosophically the most interesting of these problems is (f): the assumption that there is an entity to which a given word refers when the use of the word may be explained without any such assumption. Locke's best-known example of this error is the use of the words 'will' and 'understanding' (and other similar faculty words) to imply that there is something called 'the will' or 'the understanding' which performs the operations of volition or thinking, when we should properly say 'the man decides' or 'the man understands' (see chapter 8, p. 65).[10] But there are many other examples. Scientists come to assume that the 'entities' named in their favourite hypotheses (substantial forms, vegetative souls, the endeavour towards motion in atoms) really exist.[11] This error is even more prevalent with philosophical terms. Locke gives the example of 'matter' with all the controversies to which it has given rise.[12]

The result of all these difficulties to which language gives rise is that a great many disputes, particularly in philosophy, and most of all in legal or moral matters, are merely verbal. 'Amongst unthinking men who examine not scrupulously and carefully their own ideas and strip them not from the marks men use for them, there must be endless dispute, wrangling and jargon.'[13]

The ordinary use of words is vague and loose and inadequate for philosophical (or legal) accuracy. But the attempt to remedy this gives rise to volumes of controversial debate or commentary which leave things more obscure than before.[14]

Language has two uses, civil and philosophical. The civil or ordinary use is practical in its purpose and for the the most part entirely adequate for this purpose. 'A loose use of words serves them well enough in their ordinary discourses or affairs. But this is not sufficient for philosophical enquiries; knowledge and reasoning require precise determinate ideas.'[15] The 'faculty language' which attributes decisions to 'the will' and scientific discoveries to 'the understanding' misleads only philosophers engaged on philosophical problems, e.g. the freedom of the will. Locke does not wish to reform ordinary language here, 'nor do I deny that those words and the like are to have their place in the common use of languages that have made them current. It looks like too much affectation wholly to lay them by.'[16] And he observes with remarkable skill his own precept for philosophy: 'Philosophy itself, though it likes not a gaudy dress, yet when it appears in public must have so much complacency as to be clothed in the ordinary fashion and language of the country, so far as it can consist with truth and perspicuity.'[17] Few philosophers have achieved this aim so consistently.

Part Three
Ethics and Theology

12 Moral Principles

The Published Works. Locke's published works contain few references to moral theory or to the laws of nature, in which he included the basic principles of morals. Though the *Essay Concerning Human Understanding* originated in a discussion about the principles of morality and revealed religion, in which Locke and five or six of his friends 'found themselves at a stand by the difficulties that arose on every side',[1] the *Essay* itself does not deal in detail with these difficulties nor include a full enquiry on ethics. Locke intended to give morals the same kind of extended treatment afforded to other types of ideas in the *Essay* and he was urged both by friends and by critics to do this. His refusal seems to have been due to the survival of the doubts and difficulties which had launched the *Essay* and also to changes in his own views as he wrote successive drafts and published successive editions of it.

The Unpublished Works. The clues to Locke's moral theory have therefore to be sought in his unpublished MSS. The availability since 1947 of these MSS has made such a search possible and the work of Dr W. von Leyden[2] has provided an invaluable guide to them. The following account owes to him all its basic material. In the sections which follow, an attempt will be made *first* to explain the two alternative theories concerning moral principles current at Locke's time, and *secondly* to illustrate, by reference to his works, how he wavered between these two theories, and how a third theory developing late in his life cut across this traditional controversy.

I THE CURRENT THEORIES

There were in the mid-seventeenth century two extreme views concerning the status of moral principles.

On one view, moral principles are binding solely because they are expressions of the will of God. It is not necessary nor even possible to justify them by reasoning. This was the Calvinist position. When these principles were thought of as laws of nature, the view received additional support from moralists such as Suarez whose views were influenced by the dependence of law on sovereignty. 'Whatever pleases the ruler has the force of law.' A problem for this view is the epistemological one: how God's will is to be known. The answer is by revelation, either through Scripture or direct to the individual conscience. But behind this practical difficulty lay a theological problem about the relation between God's will and his wisdom, his omnipotence and his omniscience. Emphasis on sovereignty as the basis of law makes government arbitrary. On the other hand, if God's will is directed by goodness and wisdom, there are some principles which he could not will and others (including all moral principles) which he necessarily must will. He cannot will that the angles of a Eucidean triangle should together equal three right angles; and, if it is contrary to reason to take one's own life, he could not will a duty of suicide. Following this line, however, it would be possible, in principle, for human beings, by the use of reason, to discover that some action is equitable or right, and they would then know why God has willed such a principle.

This leads to the other extreme view, that moral principles are valid and binding independently of the reason which apprehends them and thus independently of God's wisdom too. God's functions as a legislator are to promulgate these principles (not to originate them) and to provide rewards or punishments for those who obey or disobey them. Men can discover what these principles are; they would be valid even if God did not exist. The authority for their validity and for the obligation to obey them is reason itself. Moral rules are either self-evident propositions or deducible by reasoning from such propositions. Ethics, therefore, is a complex of propositions, like geometry, all of whose truths are necessarily true.

A compromise between these two extreme views is possible. Reason may apprehend the truth of a moral law, but the command of God may be needed to give the law any moral authority, to explain why men should act in accordance with the law. God's command may have intrinsic binding force just because it is his command, or it may owe its authority to the sanctions of reward or punishment attached by God to its maintenance or violation.

II LOCKE'S POSITION

The compromise position indicated above was that maintained by Locke through most of his life. He thought that the propositions of morals were demonstrable, but that they were also expressions of the will of God and binding for this reason. But there are traces of both extreme views and much obvious doubt and hesitancy in presentation. To these difficulties was added the appearance late in his life of an egoistic hedonism which, if fully worked out, would have made both the traditional theories noted above untenable, and which led him, in explaining God's authority over man, to place increasing weight on divine rewards and punishments as the sole motives for obedience.

(In view of the problems created by the evidence noted above, this chapter will differ from the others in structure. Instead of taking Locke's views from his published works, it will trace their development through the unpublished sources, without which they would be hardly intelligible.)

(i) *The Two Treatises of Government*
While in general the second theory (that moral principles are truths apprehended by reason) is dominant in Locke and the first (that moral principles rest on the will of God) comes in exceptionally and indirectly, the opposite is the case with the *Treatises* (alternatively known as *Tracts*) written in 1660 and 1661.[3] In the First Treatise the opening paragraph lays down:

1. That if there were no law there would be no moral good or evil; man would have entire liberty in all his actions and everything would be indifferent.

2. That no one has a natural original power over the liberty of man but God himself, from whose authority all laws do fundamentally derive their obligation, as being either immediately enjoined by him, or framed by some human agency with authority derived from him.

3. That 'wherever God hath made known his own will either by the discoveries of reason, usually called the law of nature, or the revelations of his word, there nothing is left man but submission and obedience'.

4. That in matters not covered by the laws of God men are free.

But they may by compact invest another man with power over these matters. But, as there is a law of God enforcing fidelity in all lawful contracts, this obliges men to keep the compact they have made.

5. That 'it is the unalterable condition of society and government that every particular man must unavoidably part with this right to his liberty and entrust the magistrate with as full a power over his actions as he himself hath.'[4]

In the Second Treatise (entitled specifically *On Civil Government*) it is stated that divine law is that which, having been delivered to men by God, is a rule and pattern of living for them. As revealed by reason it is natural law; as manifest in divine revelation it is positive law. Both are 'moral' because they are 'exactly the same in their content and matter, and differ only in the manner of their promulgation and the clarity of their precepts. . . . Whatever this law reaches, either by prohibition or command, is always and everywhere necessarily good or evil'. 'The responsibility for society is entrusted to the magistrate by God' and human laws have therefore a delegated divine authority.[5] 'All laws in respect of their obligation are plainly divine, that is, no other law immediately and of itself binds the consciences of men except for the divine, since the others do not bind men by virtue of their own innate force, but by virtue of some divine precept on which they are grounded; nor are we bound to obey magistrates for any other reason than that the Lord has commanded it, saying Let every soul be in subjection to the higher powers, and that it is necessary to be subject, not only because of the wrath but also for conscience sake.'[6]

While it is clear that the basic nature of a moral rule is that it is a command of God, the other theory – that moral rules can be justified by reason – appears both in the reference to the laws of nature and also in the clash between the theory that we obey governments because God has authorised their rule and has commanded us to obey them, and the theory that civil authority is a rational necessity (the *unalterable* condition of society that men must *unavoidably* part with his liberty. . . .)

The predominance of the theory of divine will in this early work may be due to three factors: first, the influence on Locke of his early Puritan upbringing; secondly, the fact that he had not yet embarked on the life of philosophical speculation; and thirdly, the occasion of the *Treatises*, which was the establishment of political authority over religious worship and therefore suggests by analogy an authoritarian conception of moral law and also requires such a conception in order to justify the delegated authority of the magistrate.

(ii) The Essays on the Law of Nature

These essays[7] were written in 1660–64 and were Locke's lectures at Christ Church. They were clearly intended for ultimate publication, and they contain much material on which the early drafts of the *Essay Concerning Human Understanding* drew. But, in its final form, the latter work excluded almost entirely the arguments on moral theory which form the principal motif of the unpublished *Essays*. These essays are therefore the main source for Locke's views on morals.

There are two distinct enterprises with which Locke is faced. The first is to show wherein moral obligation consists, why men are under any obligation to obey natural law in general. The second is to show how natural laws are made known to men. To the first question, as we have seen, there may be two answers: (a) men have to obey natural law because it is the will of God; (b) men have to obey natural law because it is rational. Both appear in the *Essays*.

(a) Man, like the whole of nature, is subject to God's will.[8] 'Ultimately all obligation leads back to God, and we are bound to show ourselves obedient to the authority of his will, because both our being and our work depend on his will.'[9] The transition to (b) is made when it is pointed out that God's will cannot be obligatory on man unless it can be known by him. 'We are bound to something for the very reason that he under whose rule we are wills it ... but the declaration of his will delimits the obligation and the ground of our obedience; for we are not bound to anything except what a law-maker in some way has made known and proclaimed as his will.'[10] The will of God is made known to us as natural law and as positive law (i.e. by revelation). 'In fact the basis of obligation in both cases is the same, i.e. the will of a supreme Godhead. The two laws differ only in method of promulgation and in the way in which we know them: the former we know with certainty by the light of nature and from natural principles, the latter we apprehend by faith.'[11]

(b) The second answer to the problem of moral obligation is that it derives from reason. The law of nature is 'the decree of the divine will discernible by the light of nature and indicating what is and what is not in conformity with rational nature and *for this very reason* commanding or prohibiting'.[12] [My italics.] Aristotle's view is approved. 'He rightly concludes that the proper function of man is acting in conformity with reason, so much so that man must of necessity perform what reason prescribes.'[13] On this view, anyone – a pagan like Aristotle, or even an atheist – being of necessity rational (if he is not a child or an idiot) can discover and then will necessarily be bound to obey the law of nature. 'Aristotle says "A natural rule of justice is one which has the same validity everywhere." Hence it is rightly concluded that there is a law of nature, since there is a law which obtains everywhere.' But, as Locke has argued, a law cannot be obligatory unless it is promulgated. The promulgation to pagans or atheists cannot be by faith or revelation. Hence it must be through the light of nature which is part of the endowment of man as rational. The law of nature 'binds men, for it *contains in itself* all that is requisite to create an obligation. Though no doubt it is not made known in the same way as positive laws [i.e. by revelation] it is sufficiently known to men (and this is all that is needed for the purpose) because it can be perceived by the light of nature alone.'[14]

There is a possible compromise between these two views. Just as there is nothing to stop a government from enacting a law of nature as part of the civil law and attaching penalties to its infraction, so it would be possible for God to enact principles based on reason and attach penalties to their infraction. Locke appears to argue in this way. If it is asked why God should impose on men rules which reason validates, Locke has two arguments. First the obligation to obey the divine law 'seems to derive partly from the divine wisdom of the law-maker and partly from the right which the Creator has over his creation' . . . 'it is reasonable that we should do what shall please him who is omniscient and most wise'.[15] But omniscience and wisdom are rational excellences which would recognise, as our reason does, the validity of self-evident axioms and of demonstrations from them. Therefore God enacts those principles which reason justifies. And, in case this may seem a limitation on God's creative will, Locke points out that God could have created man differently. But 'since man has been made such as he is, equipped with reason and his other faculties and destined for this mode of life, there necessarily result from his inborn constitution some definite duties for him which cannot be other than they are'.[16] Other creatures, not endowed with reason, have no obligation to obey moral rules or to worship their Creator.

This compromise opens up the question whether God's enactment of rational principles does nothing to add to their authority except to attach sanctions of reward and punishment to them. The passage in which Locke deals with this issue is interesting as showing how both the extreme views maintained their hold on him.

We have *two* liabilities: first a liability to pay dutiful obedience; and secondly 'a liability to punishment'. This latter 'arises from a failure to pay dutiful obedience, so that those who refuse to be led by reason, and to own that in the matter of morals and right conduct they are subject to a superior authority, may recognise that they are constrained by force and punishment to be submissive to that authority . . . so that power compels those who cannot be moved by warnings. However, not all obligation seems to consist in, and ultimately to be limited by, that power which can coerce offenders and punish the wicked, but rather to consist in the authority and dominion which someone has over another. . . . Indeed all obligation binds conscience and lays a bond on the mind itself so that not fear of punishment but a rational apprehension of what is right puts us under an obligation.'[11]

It may be argued that there is no difficulty about a double obligation. When the law of the land discourages dangerous driving, citizens as law-abiding people have an extra reason for not driving dangerously, and this extra reason is not just fear of punishment. Consideration for others should alone be enough to make us drive carefully, and it is the fundamental reason for safe driving (since it is also the reason for the legislative enactment). But the parallel fails because, on these lines, the rationality of the moral rule would constitute its basic obligatory character on the individual and also the reason why God should enact it. Yet this reverses the order of obligation which Locke elsewhere lays down, by which the divine will is the ultimate and absolute moral authority.

The justification of these two sources of obligation (God and reason) is next to be considered. The account of obligation as submission to God's will is supported by Locke in a manner which he is careful to show is consistent with the epistemology to which he was committed on other grounds. God's existence and his commands are not truths imprinted on the minds of men from birth. (The third *Essay* is devoted to this topic and anticipates most of the argument against innate ideas which appear in Book I of the *Essay on the Human Understanding*.) Moral laws, like speculative principles, are not innate or presupposed as necessary hypotheses. The principle of contradiction – 'the first and best known principle of the sciences' – 'is not inscribed by nature as an axiom in our hearts nor taken for granted by anyone before he has either learned it from another or (which is the proper method of establishing principles) proved it to himself by induction and by observing particulars'.[18] 'Sense perception is the basis of our knowledge of the law of nature.'[19] In mathematics, too, sense perception is the foundation of all demonstration.[20] How then about moral principles?

Locke argues in more than one place that the law of nature is not based ultimately on reason. Reason is 'the faculty of the understanding which forms trains of thought and deduces proofs'.[21] But 'nothing is achieved by reason, that powerful faculty of arguing, unless there is something first posited and taken for granted. Reason makes use of these elements of knowledge to amplify and refine them, but it does not in the least establish them. It does not lay a foundation although again and again it raises a most majestic building and lifts the summits of knowledge right into the sky.'[22] Whence come these foundations? From sense experience.[23]

It has then to be established, on a basis of sense experience, that God exists and that his commands are obligatory, and then what these commands are. The first task is carried out in a way consistent with this demand. The arguments on which Locke bases the existence of God are the arguments from design and from the first mover.[24] These are discussed below. On the question of why men should obey God's commands, Locke argues that a wise creator creates nothing without purpose. The divine purpose for man (as for all creation) is to glorify God. In addition, God's specific purpose for man can be derived from consideration of man's nature. Man's faculties are given him to be exercised for the glory of God in worship and for the maintenance of society.[25] Locke also argues in more than one place that the status of God as omnipotent creator gives him absolute authority over man as over the rest of creation.[26]

But when we go on to ask how we know God's laws, there is much doubt and inconsistency in Locke. We have seen that he rejects the view that basic principles can be apprehended by reasoning. He says that the laws of nature have been called 'right reason', but this is a description of the laws themselves and not of the faculty which apprehends them.[27] Yet he also frequently refers to these laws as obligatory because 'conforming to our rational nature'.[28] 'Man must of necessity perform what reason prescribes.' 'Natural law can be known by reason.'[29]

There are two possible ways in which this contradiction can be explained. First, it may be held that the 'light of nature' which reveals natural laws to man is not itself reason, but is a faculty which is not possessed by any beings (such as animals or lunatics) not capable of reasoning. Secondly, it might be held that such natural laws as those against murder or theft are deduced by reasoning from more basic premisses (that man is made to live in society and that murder and theft are incompatible with social life) and that these premisess ultimately derive (as shown above) from the existence of God, which itself rests on reasoning based on sense experience. On this argument, moral rules would not themselves be given by the light of nature but would be in the same position as the conclusions of mathematical theorems or the answers to arithmetical problems.

But much of Locke's language is inconsistent with this solution, and he appears to think that the apprehension of moral laws does not depend on prior beliefs about the existence and nature of God. He does, in Essay VIII, refer to 'the basis of natural law' by which is meant 'some sort of groundwork on which all other and less evident precepts of the law are built and from which in some way they can be derived'. But his descriptions of this basis do not suggest propositions about the existence and nature of God, but a principle which is itself a moral rule 'a primary and fundamental law which is the standard and measure of all the other laws depending on it' – the 'principal law' which is 'the ground of less universal laws'.[30] And the problem remains as to how this 'principal law' is known to be valid.

Finally, it should be observed that in the *Essays* examples of laws of nature are given, though no clear method of justifying them or explaining how they are known is indicated. They include rules against 'theft and murder and other acts of that sort'; rules requiring 'reverence and fear of the Deity, tender affection for parents, love of one's neighbour, and other such sentiments'; the performance of worship, the consoling of a distressed neighbour, the relief of one in trouble, the feeding of the hungry; rules forbidding harm to reputation or character. All these bind all men at all times when they are relevant. Besides these there are special obligations dependent on status, duties of princes, parents, subjects, soliders, children.[31]

There are two other features of the *Essays* which deserve mention. The first (which is important in view of the hedonistic theory which Locke came later to elaborate) occurs in Essay VIII which is devoted to proving that self-interest cannot be the basis of the law of nature. The second is Locke's vivid recognition of the variety of moral standards which his interest in books of travel had led him to appreciate. This enables him to reject social custom (or 'tradition') as a basis for the law of nature. But it also leaves him with the problem how, if man's faculties enable him to apprehend the law of nature, such variations can arise and be explained. Variations are perpetuated because most men are satisfied to live by second-hand opinion and therefore to accept the mores of their society without question, and because education is given almost entirely in terms of the tradition of the society.[32]

But how should moral principles which diverge from the law of nature ever become accepted in the first place? Locke anaswers: 'Because men are either carried off by inveterate habit, or led aside by their passions, thus yielding to the morality of others; also they follow the herd in the manner of brute beasts, since they do not allow themselves the use of their reason, but give way to appetite. In like manner, in fact, he who will not open his eyes, as well as he who is born blind, is liable to errors'.[33] But 'inveterate habit', 'the morality of others' and the following of the herd do not explain why such morality should be first adopted, but only how it is perpetuated. And appetite normally leads men to flout conventions and not to hold moral rules which diverge from nature. Blindness too will explain the non-recognition of a true rule, but it does not explain the recognition of a false one. Thus, while Locke's recognition of variation is honest and remarkable at his time, his explanations of it are unconvincing.

(iii) Drafts of the Essay Concerning Human Understanding
In 1671 occurred the meeting with five or six of Locke's friends which gave rise to the great *Essay Concerning Human Understanding*. The discussion concerned the principles of morality and revealed religion, and the difficulties which arose led Locke to start his

enquiry into the nature and extent of human knowledge. Two drafts of the *Essay*, dating from 1671, have survived, in both of which much material from the *Essays on the Law of Nature* was embodied. This material, however, is almost entirely epistemological, and moral issues are excluded, with the obvious intention of later treatment in another work. 'Because we cannot come to a certain knowledge of those rules of our actions [sc. moral rules] without first making known a lawgiver with power and will to reward and punish, and secondly without showing how he has declared his will and law, I must at present only suppose this rule till a fit place to speak of those, God, the law of nature, and revelation, and only at present mention what is to our present purpose.'[34] The drafts both contain arguments for the existence of God, but nothing on ethics or the law of nature.

The next landmark in the development of Locke's views on conduct is the entry in the *Journal* for 16 July 1676 on "Pleasure, Pain and the Passions".[35] This entry is the first appearance of the hedonistic theory of action which occurs in the *Essay*[36] and cuts across the moral theories so far discussed. Pleasure and pain are 'two roots out of which all passions spring, and a centre on which they all turn. Where they are removed the passions would all cease, having nothing left to wind them up or set them going.' 'Several things are apt to produce pleasure and pain.' Roses, wine, light, liberty, power, knowledge, children and grandchildren please most men. 'So that wherever anything offers itself to the understanding as capable to produce pleasure, there it constantly and immediately produces love, which seems to be nothing but the consideration or having in the mind the idea of some thing that is able in some way of application to produce delight or pleasure in us.'[37] The argument here is that we love what we believe *will produce* pleasure in us. The pleasure is *anticipated* pleasure. But there is the hint of a transition to another view, when Locke deals with hatred. 'Hatred is . . . the *presence* of an idea considered as naturally disposed to disease and vex us.'[38] [My italics.] So far it is *anticipated* vexation which gives rise to hatred. But, when Locke explains why hate is more violent than love, he says this is 'because the sense of evil or pain works more upon us than that of good or pleasure; we bear the absence of a great pleasure more easily than the presence of a little pain'.[39] It might be held that 'presence' here means 'anticipated presence'. But the transition is certainly noticeable later when he says: 'The mind finding in itself the ideas of several objects which if enjoyed would produce pleasure . . . and the possibility of . . . doing something toward the procuring the enjoyment of that good, observes in itself some uneasiness or trouble or displeasure till it be done and this is what we call desire, so that desire seems to me to be a pain the mind is in till some good . . . which it judges possible and seasonable, be obtained.'[40] If it is now asked how human actions are determined, the first answer – that they are determined by the pleasure anticipated from their results – would seem to give way to a second: that they are determined by the pain of unsatisfied desire. The implication of either of these conclusions for moral theory are not drawn out in the *Journal*, but they are obvious enough. It is not explicitly stated that pleasure and pain determine *all* our actions, but only that they determine our passions; but the question of moral motivation is inevitable and the developments in this direction will concern us in the rest of this chapter. Another entry in the *Journal* (15 July 1678)[41] shows Locke maintaining one of the methods suggested above (p. 110) for showing that moral rules are demonstrable, as deducible from the nature of God. 'If he finds that God has made him and all other men in a state wherein they cannot subsist without society, and has given them judgment to discern what is capable of preserving that society, can he but conclude that he is obliged and that God requires him to follow those rules which conduce to the preserving of society?'[42]

The last unpublished paper which is relevant to the present purpose is entitled *Of Ethick in General*.[43] Dr von Leyden shows that it was intended to become chapter xxi of Book IV of the *Essay*, and that it was written on the eve of its publication. He adds that it provides a comprehensive account of Locke's thoughts on morality, an account much needed owing to the scattered and inconsistent references to ethics in the *Essay*.[44] Yet it was not included when the *Essay* was published. There can be little doubt that this was due to the further development in it of the hedonistic theory first appearing in 1676. We noted in dealing with this first appearance that 'the passions' were said to be determined by pleasure and pain but that nothing was said about moral motivation (see above paragraph). Now, however, the next step is taken. Moral good or evil derives its name from a tendency in objects to produce pleasure or pain in a person, by the intervention of his will.[45] Professor Aaron[46] thinks the last phrase refers to the intervention of God's will, through divine rewards and punishments. But Dr von Leyden remarks with justice that the will referred to in the context is that of 'an intelligent free agent' that is, a human being, not God.[47] On the other hand it is not at all clear how the intervention of a human will can give rise to a tendency in objects to produce pleasure.

A clue might be sought in a MS. note of uncertain date quoted by Cranston: 'It is a man's proper business to seek happiness and avoid misery . . . I will therefore make it my business to seek satisfaction and delight and avoid uneasiness and disquiet.'[48] But the note goes on to say that there are certain lasting pleasures which should not be sacrificed to immediate or short-term pleasures. They include health, reputation, knowledge, doing good and the expectation of eternal happiness. Now the intervention of the human will might be required to prefer a lasting to an immediate pleasure. Thus 'doing good' gives lasting pleasure and 'the expectation of eternal happiness' does so too. Aaron's point is met, because eternal happiness ensues on moral rectitude only because of God's will rewarding moral actions. Yet it is the intervention of the human will which prefers the lasting pleasure of expectation thus aroused to the more immediate pleasures. A passage from *Of Ethick in General* which Locke deleted would confirm this interpretation: 'Moral rectitude, which when considered is but conformity to the natural law of God, would signify nothing and moral goodness be no reason to direct my action, were there not really pleasure that would follow from the doing of it and pain avoided greater than is to be found in the action itself.'[49]

Despite these hedonistic tendencies, the paper *Of Ethick in General* concludes by repeating the passage quoted above from Draft A saying that we must suppose a lawgiver with authority and a right to ordain and a power to reward and punish.[50] The paper adds that the existence of such a lawgiver has been already proved and 'the next thing is to show that there are certain rules, certain dictates, which it is his will that all men should conform their action to, and that this will of his is sufficiently promulgated and made known to all mankind'.[51] But there the paper ends.

We may now sum up the position as it seems to have stood before the publication of the *Essay*. Moral conduct is conduct according to a rule. These rules are expressions of the will of God, who has supreme authority over all creation including man. But man, as a rational being cannot have a duty to obey rules unless he is aware of them. They must therefore be promulgated. This is achieved either by revelation or by the light of nature. Revelation operates through Scripture and is therefore available only to Christian believers. The light of nature is a possession of all rational beings and therefore is available to all men everywhere Thus we can come to know what is right and wrong. But the only motive for action which a man can have is the pursuit of pleasure or the avoidance of pain. Thus a man will not do what is right unless he believes that this choice will bring him in the end more pleasure than pain.

(iv) The Essay Concerning Human Understanding.

We now turn from the unpublished works of Locke to examine what he had to say on ethics to the readers of his own time.

The subject first appears in Book I where he rejects the idea of innate truth in morals. This he argues from the lack of any general assent to any moral rule, and from the fact that 'there cannot any one moral rule be proposed whereof a man may not justly demand a reason'.[52] 'These moral rules then are capable of demonstration and therefore it is our own fault if we come not to a certain knowledge of them.'[53]

The claim that moral rules are demonstrably certain recurs, later, in Book IV, where their status is equated with that of the truths of mathematics. As shown above (chapter 10, p. 81), Locke held that mathematical truth is purely hypothetical. It is attained by the apprehension of necessary connections between man-made general ideas, whch need have no instantiation in the real world. 'Hence it follows that moral knowledge is as capable of real certainty as mathematics; for certainty being nothing but the perception of the agreement or disagreement of our ideas, and demonstration being nothing but the perception of such agreement by the intervention of other ideas or mediums. . . .'[54] The point about independence of real existence is made clear in Book III. 'Mixed modes, especially those belonging to morality, being most of them such combinations of ideas as the mind puts together of its own choice, and whereof there are not always standing patterns to be found existing . . . men may, if they please, exactly know the ideas that go to each composition.'[55] 'Upon this ground it is that I am bold to think that morality is capable of demonstration as well as mathematics, since the precise real essence of the things moral words stand for may be perfectly known, and so the congruity

116

and incongruity of the things themselves be certainly discovered, in which consists perfect knowledge.'[56] We can know for certain the truth of mathematical propositions about squares and circles, regardless of the facts that there may be no examples of perfect squareness or circularity in the real world and that if there were we could never *know* it was so. 'Nor are Tully's Offices less true because there is nobody in the world that exactly practises his rules and lives up to that pattern of a virtuous man which he has given us and which existed nowhere when he writ, but in idea.'[57]

In the passages to which reference has been made above Locke gives some examples of necessary connection in morals:

- (*a*) Any rational being is subject to law.[58]
- (*b*) Violation of property is unjust, and
- (*c*) No government can allow absolute liberty.[59]
- (*d*) Murder deserves death.[60]
- (*e*) Theft is unjust.[61]

In the case of example (*c*) the necessary connection is apprehended through the mediation of the idea of law. Government implies rules or laws, and laws are incompatible with absolute liberty. In all the other cases, it appears that the necessary connection is directly apprehended when the ideas in question are clearly defined. This is explicitly claimed for (*b*) and (*e*). The idea of property is a right to something and the invasion of a right is unjust or, in other words, 'taking from others without their consent what their honest industry has possessed them of' is unjust. Hence men should be careful to get their moral terms clear and distinct and to define them exactly on occasion.[62]

There would seem to be something unsystematic about this ideal of moral demonstration. Moral truth would be a collection of apprehended necessary connections with no relations to each other except within particular chains of demonstration. One way of achieving a systematic unity is excluded by Locke's parallel with mathematics. Aristotle thought that mathematical truths had to be deduced from a limited number of first principles known intuitively to be true. As we have seen (chapter 10, p. 82) Locke rejected this for mathematics and would presumably reject it for moral demonstration also. To say that these demonstrations are purely hypothetical is to say that no question arises about the truth or falsehood of the connected propositions taken in isolation (or, in Locke's language, about the application to particular substances of the ideas related in these propositions).

While there would be general acceptance of Locke's account of the epistemological status of mathematics, his corresponding claim for moral truth was queried in his own day and would be rejected by modern philosophers. Locke himself was aware of this, and gives some reasons to explain why it was thought that moral rules were not demonstrable, and why it is less easy to see that they are so than it is in mathematics. First, mathematicians can use diagrams to represent the ideas with which a demonstration is concerned, and the diagram has a visual relationship to the idea. In morals the ideas are signified by words which are arbitrarily chosen and in themselves give no clue to the nature of the idea signified. Secondly, ideas in morals are more complex than in mathematics, with the result that different men can give different meanings to the same word and one man may find it difficult, in the course of a long argument, to retain the signification of his words unaltered, or to be sure he has done so. The mathematician avoids this danger by his use of symbols, arithmetical or algebraical, which he can use to fix the signification of his terms.[63]

Locke was frequently urged, both by friends, and by critics of the *Essay* to provide a systematic demonstration of moral truths. His friend, James Tyrrell, repeatedly urged him, both before and after the publication of the *Essay*, to publish the *Essays on the Law of Nature*. Such a publication 'would make a second part to the former work'. This had certainly been Locke's intention, but he seems to have lost interest or confidence in it during the years when he was engaged in practical affairs.[64] Tyrrell himself published a work on the law of nature in 1692, in which he acknowledges a debt to Locke's *Essay* of 1690, but in which can also be traced considerable borrowings from Locke's unpublished *Essays on the Law of Nature*. Dr von Leyden thinks that Tyrrell's long acquaintance with the *Essays* in manuscript, and some confusion concerning the sources he used, resulted in unconscious plagiarism here.[65]

A critic, Thomas Burnet, in his *Remarks on the Essay* (1697) asked on what foundation Locke would build the moral law when he set about to demonstrate it. In a brief reply to him Locke wrote: 'I have indeed said in my book that I thought morality capable of demonstration as well as the mathematics, but I do not remember where I promised this gentleman to demonstrate it to him.'[66] This is the fair point that the *Essay* is an epistemological treatise and need only show in general how moral truth is attained. It need not contain a demonstration of morals any more than it need include mathematical theorems.

Burnet went on to argue that, even if moral truth could be demonstrated, this would be no use to ordinary men who 'must have a more compendious way to know their duty than by long deductions'. Locke leaves this point unanswered; but the obvious answer, which appears in the *Essays*, is that ordinary men do not *know* their duty. They have beliefs about it, mainly derived from tradition and their social environment. In answer to the demand for a 'foundation', Locke replies: 'Whoever sincerely acknowledges any law to be the law of God cannot fail to acknowledge also that it hath all the reason and ground that a just law can or ought to have.' This line of defence will concern us in the sections which follow.

The most interesting exchanges on this issue occur in Locke's correspondence with his friend, William Molyneux, in 1692 and 1696 after the publication of the *Essay*. Molyneux insisted that Locke should 'think of obliging the world with a treatise of morals drawn up according to the hints you frequently give in your Essay, of being demonstrable, according to the mathematical method'.[67] Locke in his reply says

> Though by the view I had of moral ideas while I was considering that subject, I thought I saw that morality might be demonstratively made out; yet whether I am able so to make it out is another question. Everyone could not have demonstrated what Mr Newton's book hath shown to be demonstrable: but to show my readiness to obey your commands, I shall not decline the first leisure I can get to employ some thoughts that way; unless I find what I have said in my Essay shall have stirred up some abler man to prevent me, and effectually do that service to the world.[68]

Molyneux returned to the charge. Locke admitted that others besides Molyneux had urged the same task upon him, and says he had not wholly laid by the thoughts of it, and had collected some materials for it, as they occurred to him. But, he doubted whether it was prudent, in one of his age and health, to set about the task. 'Did the world want a rule, I confess there could be no work so necessary, nor so commendable. But the Gospel contains so perfect a body of ethics that reason may be excused from that inquiry, since she may find man's duty clearer and easier in revelation than in herself.'[69]

Thus reason yields to revelation as the authority for moral rules. Yet a difficulty still remains. Revelation comes to us through the New Testament, and particularly the Gospels, and these texts may not be unambiguously clear. 'Though everything said in the text be infallibly true, yet the reader may be – nay, cannot choose but be very fallible in the understanding of it.' While 'the precepts of natural religion are plain and very intelligible to all mankind and seldom come to be controverted; and other revealed truths which are conveyed to us by books and languages are liable to the difficulties incident to words: methinks it would become us to be more careful and diligent in observing the former and less magisterial, positive and imperious in imposing our own sense and interpretations of the latter'.[70] It would seem that, for interpretation of the Gospel, we are again driven back on human reason, though perhaps this task is less formidable than *a priori* demonstration of a system of moral rules.

We have so far considered the claim in the *Essay* that moral truth is demonstrable in the same way as mathematics. It might well be asked how, in that case, is there any connection between moral truth and actual conduct or reality. In mathematics, the answer is that if two ideas are necessarily connected, and if, in the real world, there happens to be a thing corresponding to one of these ideas then the other will also be exemplified in reality. So in morality, theft and injustice are necessarily connected ideas; and if there is anywhere an actual instance of theft there will also be an actual instance of injustice. We have proceeded from a hypothetical connection to an actual connection.

But we still have to find out what this has to do with action or *duty*. The fact that an actual (approximately) triangular area will have angles which total (approximately) two right angles provides no reason for action. Why should the fact that an actual instance of theft will also be an instance of injustice do so?

In Locke's last published work, *The Reasonableness of Christianity* (1695), he states frankly the failure of human reason to provide moral demonstrations of natural law, and he adds the point now under consideration that even if such rational laws were obtainable they would not explain moral obligation.

It would seem, by the little that has hitherto been done in it, that it is too hard a task for unassisted reason to establish morality in all its parts, upon its true foundation with a clear and convincing light.[71]

It is plain that human reason unassisted failed men in its great and proper business of morality. It never from unquestionable principles, by clear deductions, made out an entire body of the law of nature.[72]

[But] what would this amount to, towards being a steady rule, a certain transcript of a law we are under? . . . mankind might hearken to it, or reject it, as they pleased; or as it suited their interest, passions, principles, or humours. They were under no obligation.[73]

The answer to this question is that revelation provides not only clear answers to the problems of right and wrong, but also an absolute authority to oblige men to action. 'Such a law of morality Jesus Christ hath given us in the New Testament by revelation. . . . Here morality has a sure standard that revelation vouches and reason cannot gainsay nor question; but both together witness to come from God the great law-maker.'[74]

Moral rules are obligatory then because they are the revealed commands of God.

The formulation 'it is right' or 'it is a duty' conceals the prescriptive character of these rules. They are not true or false. 'For "Parents preserve your children" is . . . no truth at all, it being a command and not a proposition and not capable of truth or falsehood. To make it capable of being assented to as true, it must be reduced to some such proposition as this, "It is the duty of parents to preserve their children".'[75]

This, however, might still seem to be a hypothetical connection. If there is a God, and if he has commanded certain actions, we ought to perform them. But here Locke thinks he can break out of the hypothetical network. For he can demonstrate that God exists; 'no existence of anything without us but only of God can be certainly known further than our senses inform us . . . so having the idea of God and myself, of fear and obedience, I cannot but be sure that God is to be feared and obeyed by me'.[76]

The argument for God's existence is considered in chapter 13. There are two difficulties in the rest of the inference. The duties to honour and fear God might be defended as following from his nature as infinate power and wisdom. But we cannot *obey* God until we know his commands. In the paper *Of Ethick in General*, Locke had laid down that moral theory should consider 'species of action in the world, as justice, temperance, fortitude, drunkenness, and theft . . . the end and use of morality being to direct our lives and, by showing us what actions are good and what bad, prepare us to do the one and avoid the other'.[77] But it is precisely this demonstration by rational means which Locke had come to doubt. And his reply to Molyneux that reason was unnecessary since revelation provided so clear an answer, was, as we have seen, echoed in his last published work. But this answer has the drawback that *knowledge* of moral obligation would be limited to those of Christian faith.

The second question posed by the argument from God to moral duty is the question why men should obey God's laws. One answer, as we have seen, lies in the nature of the relation between God and man. God has a right to our obedience: 'we are his creatures'.[78] 'He also that hath the idea of an intelligent but frail and weak being, made by and dependent on another, who is eternal, omnipotent, perfectly wise and good, will as certainly know that man is to honour fear and obey God, as that the sun shines when he sees it.'[79] The other answer emerges from the hedonistic vein in Locke's thinking, which, as we have seen, was a late development. To the appearances of this hedonistic view in the *Essay* we now turn.

Locke repeatedly asserts that pleasure and pain are the only motives for action, 'beyond which we have no concernment, either of knowing or being'.[80] 'Things are good or evil only in reference to pleasure or pain. That we call good, which is apt to cause or increase pleasure, or diminish pain in us, or else to procure or preserve us the possession of any other good or absence of any evil.'[81] 'Pleasure and pain, and that which causes them, good and evil, are the hinges on which our passions turn.'[82] In the first edition of the *Essay* Locke held that the passions were moved by the anticipation of expected pleasure or pain. But in the second edition he maintained that desire is itself a state of uneasiness or pain and it is this pain which moves to action. 'Good and evil, present or absent, it is true work upon the mind, but that which immediately determines the will, from time to time, to every voluntary action is the uneasiness of desire fixed on some absent good.'[83] This uneasiness, however, is not the only spur to action,[84] for two reasons. First, because 'the motive for continuing in the same action is the present satisfaction in it';[85] and secondly, because a man has the power to suspend action, due to a present uneasiness, while he considers the consequences and circumstances of the proposed action.[86] But nothing will alter the direction of his action except a greater uneasiness due to the discovery or contemplation of such consequences. It would therefore seem that 'the most pressing uneasiness naturally determines the will'.[87]

Yet Locke also maintains that the greatest good is not always desired, though his method of dealing with this crucial issue in morals (crucial especially for a Utilitarian) is far from satisfactory. 'All good, even seen and confessed to be so, does not necessarily move every particular man's desire.'[88] How is it possible for the greatest good, seen to be so (i.e. seen to be productive of the greatest possible pleasure for the agent), not to determine the will? First, other people may find pleasure in knowledge and deem it good, though I do not; secondly, on most occasions I may find more pleasure in thinking than in eating (and therefore say that thinking is a greater good) but at the moment hunger makes the desire to eat more pressing; thirdly, pain or disease may warp our judgment about future pleasures, as may distance in time, and countless other causes.[89] But all this argument implies that, at the time of action, my judgement is mistaken and therefore that I do what I wrongly believe will bring me most happiness or relief from pain. How can this be reconciled with Locke's assertion that 'all good both seen and confessed to be so does not necessarily move every particular man's desire', that 'men may have a clear view of good, great and confessed good, without being concerned for it or moved by it',[90] that 'satisfied of the possibility of a perfect, secure, and lasting happiness in a future state . . . their desires are not moved by this greater apparent good'?[91]

Locke does not make it clear how he escapes this difficulty; and indeed, so long as he maintained the theory of his first edition that the motive of an action is always the greatest good in prospect, he could not escape it. But the view that appears in the second edition gives him the necessary loophole. The belief that something would give me future pleasure may arouse no desire at all or a desire so weak as to be easily over-ridden by more immediate aims. The desire aroused is not (except in a wholly rational creature) proportionate to the pleasure believed to be obtainable. 'Absent good though thought on, confessed, and appearing to be good, not making any part of this unhappiness in its absence, is justled out, to make way for the removal of those uneasinesses we feel.'[92] In this connection, Locke also recognises the distinction between believing a pleasure will ensue and acutely feeling its absence. We may believe children are being starved in a civil war, but the likelihood of this belief affecting our action will vary as the source varies; a newspaper report, photographs or films, a visit to the scene. So, with absent good, 'due and repeated contemplation' is needed to bring it nearer to our mind, give us some relish for it, and raise in us some desire.[93] But the main source of false judgement still remains the distance in time of the good or evil consequences which fail to move us as they should. 'Were the pleasure of drinking accompanied the very moment a man takes off his glass with that sick stomach and aching head which, in some men, are sure to follow not many hours after; I think that nobody, whatever pleasure he had in his cups, would on these conditions ever let wine touch his lips; which yet he daily swallows, and the evil side comes to be chosen only by the fallacy of a little difference in time.'[94]

In view of all this, how can moral obligations bind a man? When immediate desires have the greatest urgency, when the claims of others are so easily rejected, when most moral duties seem to require self-control or self-sacrifice, how are they to be recommended to a being whose final decision in any situation is determined by his last judgment of his own happiness, his maximum pleasure and avoidance of pain? Locke's answer is an appeal to divine rewards and punishments. We have seen how the hypothetical connection between moral obligation and God's will is made actual by the proof of God's existence. But if a human being asks, 'Why should I obey God's will?' the answer (as in the field of human law) must be 'crime doesn't pay'. 'That men should keep their compacts is certainly a great and undeniable rule in morality. But yet, if a Christian, who has the view of happiness and misery in another life, be asked why a man should keep his word, he will give this as a reason: Because God, who has the power of eternal life and death, requires it of us.'[95] The true ground of morality 'can only be the will and law of a God who sees men in the dark, has in his hands rewards and punishments, and power enough to call to account the proudest offender'.[96]

It might be thought that Locke leaves open here the possibility that good men might obey the moral rules because of the 'moral and eternal obligation which these rules evidently have'.[97] 'Crime doesn't pay' is addressed not to the ordinary citizen but to the potential criminal. We recall that in the *Essays on the Law of Nature* Locke maintained that punishment and reward are not the basic, reasons why men obey the law of nature. Conscience is the normal motive (see p. 106). But his hedonistic theory had, by the time he wrote the *Essay*, gained such a grip on him that this loophole seems now to be blocked. 'What duty is, cannot be understood without a law, nor a law be known or supposed without a law-maker, or without reward and punishment.'[98] 'Moral laws are set as a curb and restraint to these exorbitant desires, which they cannot be but by rewards and punishments, that will overbalance the satisfaction anyone shall propose to himself in the breach of the law.'[99]

> Good and evil, as hath been shown, are nothing but pleasure or pain or that which occasions or procures pleasure or pain to us. Moral good and evil, then, is only the conformity or disagreement of our voluntary actions to some law whereby good or evil is drawn on us by the will and power of the law-maker; which good and evil, pleasure or pain, attending our observance or breach of the law by the decree of the law-maker, is that we call reward and punishment.[100]

Men 'judge of the . . . moral good or evil of their actions: that is, whether, as duties or sins, they are likely to procure them happiness or misery from the hands of the Almighty'.[101]

Why should Locke not maintain, as he had in the *Essays*, that conscience is the proper motive for obedience to God, and that rewards and punishments are a secondary consideration? It seems likely that this is because the evidence of the vagaries of conscience, both among the fanatical sects in England and, as reported by travellers, among pagans throughout the world, had convinced him that no reliance could be placed on conscience as a guide to moral truth. Conscience is 'nothing but our own opinion or judgment on the moral rectitude or pravity of our own actions'[102] – a definition which is followed by two paragraphs of examples of the actions conscience has been found to endorse, from cannibalism to extremes of sexual perversion.

In any case how, for an egoistic hedonist, could conscience itself provide a motive for action? There is a loophole which does appear once in the *Essay*: 'Let a man be ever so well persuaded of the advantages of virtue . . . yet, till he hungers or thirsts after righteousness, till he feels an uneasiness in the want of it, his will will not be determined to any action in pursuit of this confessed greater good.'[103] But the main weight falls on the theory of rewards and punishments, and indeed Locke devotes greater space to hammering home this point than he does to any other single argument in the *Essay*.[104]

Since, however, it is clear that virtue and vice are not always suitably requited in this life, the idea of moral conduct must depend on rewards and punishments in a future life. Locke endorses the judgment of St Paul, with which the Burial Service has made us so familiar. 'For if there be no prospect beyond the grave, the inference is certainly right, "Let us eat and drink", let us enjoy what we delight in, "for tomorrow we shall die".'[105]

There seems here a clash between the notion of morality as the expression, through reason and revelation, of unchanging and demonstrable laws, having intrinsic obligation on men as expressions of the will of God, on the one hand, and the egoistic hedonism of the theory of divine retribution on the other. There is no clear solution to this problem, and there can be no doubt that this, added to the difficulties of demonstration of moral rules, reinforced Locke's reluctance to publish a work on ethics.

(v) *Locke's Final View*

There is a possible compromise between the two extremes noted above, and it is one suggested by a difficulty in which Utilitarians themselves were entangled, the difficulty of reconciling the obligation to do what will promote the greatest happiness of the greatest number with the psychological 'fact' that every human being pursues *his own* happiness and can pursue no other end. Mill, as is well known, reconciled these two principles by a series of logical fallacies. But the parallel for Locke is to be found in Bentham:

The happiness of the individuals, of whom a community is composed, that is their pleasures and security, is the end and the sole end which the legislator ought to have in view: the sole standard in conformity to which each individual ought, as far as depends on the legislator, to be *made* to fashion his behaviour. But whether it be this or anything else that is to be *done*, there is nothing by which a man can be *made* to do it, but either pain or pleasure.[106] [Italics in original]

The sources of pain and pleasure which can be used to *make* individuals take account of the general happiness are termed 'sanctions': physical, political, moral, and religious, according as the source of the 'sanction' is a natural cause independent of human will, the arm of the law, public opinion (from 'moral' referring to '*mores*' or customs) or the hand of God. Bishop Butler, who devotes the main argument of his moral writing to a defence of the absolute and supreme authority of conscience, appears to admit in one isolated passage the same difficulty and urge the same solution. 'Let it be allowed, though virtue or moral rectitude does indeed consist in affection to and pursuit of what is right and good as such; yet that when we sit down in a cool hour, we can neither justify to ourselves this or any other pursuit, till we are convinced that it will be for our happiness or at least not contrary to it.'[107]

There are indeed indications in Locke's last work, *The Reasonableness of Christianity*, that this was his final view. He argues that 'it is too hard a task for unassisted reason to establish morality in all its parts upon a true foundation with a clear and convincing light'.[108] and that therefore the revelation of God's commands in Scripture is the only reliable source for moral principles. But the Christian revelation included more than the moral law. Its promise of rewards for virtue made the practice of virtue reasonable. 'Manknd who are and must be allowed to pursue their happiness, nay, cannot be hindered; could not but think themselves excused from a strict observation of rules which appeared so little to consist of their chief end, happiness'.[109] The pagan philosophers made the chief of their arguments the excellency of virtue. But ordinary men remained unmoved by this.

> The philosophers indeed showed the beauty of virtue . . . but, leaving her unendowed, very few were willing to espouse her. The generality could not refuse her their esteem and commendation, but still turned their back on her and forsook her as a match not for their turn. But now there being put into the scales on her side 'an exceeding and immortal weight of glory', interest is come about to her, and virtue is now visibly the most enriching purchase and by much the best bargain. That

she is the perfection and excellency of our nature, that she is herself a reward and will recommend our names to future ages, is not all that can now be said of her. It is not strange that the learned heathen satisfied not many with these airy commendations. It has another relish and efficacy to persuade men that if they live well here they shall be happy hereafter.... The view of heaven and hell will cast a slight upon the short pleasures and pains of this present state, and give attractions and encouragements to virtue, which reason and interest and the care of ourselves cannot but allow and prefer. Upon this foundation and upon this only, morality stands firm and may defy all competition. This makes it more than a name; a substantial good, worth all our aims and endeavours; and thus the Gospel of Jesus Christ has delivered it to us.[110]

III Comment

Modern philosophers would, in general, follow Hume in rejecting the view that morals can be based on reason, and in maintaining that issues of truth and falsehood do not arise in morals. Locke indeed indicates one line which such moralists have taken when he says that moral principles are really commands and that 'true' and 'false' do not apply to commands (see above, p. 121). But the further conclusion that there is no question of objectivity in moral standards does not follow for Locke, because, for him, moral principles are God's commands and there is a real question whether (e.g.) monogamy or euthanasia is enjoined by God. For the modern imperativist (e.g. C. L. Stevenson or R. M. Hare) the command is that of the person pronouncing the moral judgement, and therefore no question of objectivity arises.

Locke's problems, however, still remain pressing for the theologian, and the evaluation of the sources for moral judgement: conscience, Scripture, tradition, and authority, remains a source of difference between the churches. Only among Roman Catholic theologians (such as Maritain) can be found surviving a belief in natural law or the voice of reason in morals.

13 Theology and Religion

(i) The Existence of God

Locke argues that the idea of God is not innate, because children and many races of men do not have it;[1] and because among those who do have it there are many different ideas of God.[2] Thus 'the truest and best notions men had of God were not imprinted but acquired by thought and meditation and a right use of their faculties'.[3]

This 'adequate' idea of God is for Locke 'the idea of a supreme Being, infinite in power and goodness, whose workmanship we are and on whom we depend'.[4] It is attained by 'enlarging' all the ideas we have about spirits from reflection on our own nature (i.e. by introspection) with the idea we have of infinity. Thus we attain the idea of a Being of infinite duration, power and knowledge whom we rightly call 'God'.[5]

But how do we proceed from this idea to reality? How do we know that anything independent of our minds corresponds to this idea? The passage cited above from Book II includes existence with duration, power and knowledge as among the ideas about ourselves obtained through introspection and enlarged to infinity to obtain the idea of God. We have also seen earlier (chapter 6, p. 56) that, in the case of ideas of reflection, the problem of correspondence between idea and reality did not arise for Locke. Introspection is infallible. When I have *by introspection* the idea of pain, I really am in pain. When I have the idea that someone else is in pain, his pain is problematic and at best probable. Therefore also I am aware that I exist, and this is certain.

It might be supposed from this that when Locke attributes existence along with infinite power and knowledge to God he is claiming certainty that God exists. This would be the ontological argument, that the idea of God includes existence. But Locke rejects this argument,[6] and his rejection is quite consistent with his account of our idea of God. There are people whose idea of the Loch Ness monster 'includes existence' and people whose idea does not, as there are theists and atheists. It is of course true that the upholders of the ontological argument would make 'existence' carry a special meaning in relation to God; and true also that the implication in 'the idea of existence' that existence is an attribute is questionable. But all I am arguing here is that Locke is consistent in saying that our idea of God includes existence (however that may be analysed) and in rejecting the ontological argument.

Locke's own argument is the causal argument, though there are occasional suggestions also of the argument from design. I am aware by immediate intuition of my own existence. But everything existent must have a cause, and the cause must be adequate to produce the effect. A mind cannot be produced by a purely material cause. Hence the cause of my existence must be a 'cogitative being'. Locke has argued that it is inconceivable that there was a time when nothing existed and therefore that something has existed from eternity. It follows that this eternal being is a cogitative being. And, since it must be adequate to produce all the perfections which can ever after exist, it must include infinite wisdom and power.[7]

The weaknesses of this argument are obvious. First, it does not follow from the premiss that there cannot have been a time when nothing existed that something has existed from eternity. For the alternative is that at any time there have existed temporal events. Secondly, it does not follow from the principle of causation that there must be a first cause. Locke's original account of the idea of infinity[8] is the negative one that one can go on multiplying numbers or extending our idea of distance without limit. From which it would follow that every event has a cause, but there is no first cause. Thirdly, the causal principle is taken as a self-evident truth (Cf. chapter 4, p. 39). Fourthly, it does not follow that the cause of all existent beings is a single being. Indeed, so far as the causal principle is to be regarded as the basic assumption for scientific enquiry, the opposite is the case. Of course it may be argued that many existent causes limit each other and the demands for *perfection* and *omnipotence* require a single cause, just as the quarrels on Olympus helped the case for monotheism. But no such argument is to be found in Locke.

We have seen how the goodness of God is inferred from the causal argument that every perfection must have an adequate cause. The argument from design is another route to the same conclusion. The intricacy of nature and its capacity to serve man's well-being give evidence of the wisdom and benevolence of its creator. Traces of this argument too may be found in Locke. Material causes 'could never produce that order, harmony, and beauty which are to be found in nature'.[9] 'The visible marks of extraordinary wisdom and power appear so plainly in all the works of the creation that a rational creature who will but seriously reflect on them cannot miss the discovery of a Deity.'[10] The benevolence of God is shown by the way in which he has fitted our senses for their task of discriminating items in our environment, through the ideas of secondary qualities (Cf. chapter 2, p. 26). Stillingfleet criticises Locke's omission of the ontological argument.[11] But Locke replies[12] that the ontological argument depends on the Cartesian principle that truth lies in clear and distinct ideas, which he rejects, and that there is no reason to suppose (as Kant later argued) that, without the ontological argument, the other arguments are invalid.

(ii) Religious Beliefs

Locke lived in a time of intense religious controversy. With his interest in epistemology, he naturally took the main differences between the sects to be in the methods by which their doctrines and practices were defined and defended rather than in the doctrines themselves.

From this point of view it may be said that there were five main trends, though they shaded into each other and any particular sect might be hard to fit in to such a classification. 1. There was the Roman Catholic Church, owing its doctrine and practice to papal authority. 2. There was the Church of England, under episcopal discipline, and owing its doctrine mainly to tradition. It was divided, then as now, into a 'high church' wing approximating at its extreme to Roman practice and a 'low church' wing approximating to the more 'moderate' Protestant sects. 3. There were the Protestant reformers, relying on Scripture for doctrine and practice. 4. There were the sects which relied on an 'inner light' as guide in religion and morals, and therefore rejected both ecclesiastical authority and the infallibility of Scripture in favour of a direct personal revelation. Of these the Quakers, led by George Fox, were the most important. 5. There were those who were impressed by the insoluble conflicts presented by the other four and by the triumphs of reason in mathematics and science, and who therefore hoped to establish a 'natural religion' based on human reason. They held that reason could justify the existence of God and his concern with the world, the moral law, and reward and punishment. They tended to reject the divinity of Christ, the doctrine of the Trinity, the occurrence of miracles and the infallibility of Scripture. The main sects here, in the order of their emergence, were the Socinians, the Unitarians, and the Deists. Locke's reaction to these various claims can be traced in the following account of his position.

For Locke, the truths of religion other than the demonstrable existence of God rest on faith not reason, and the faith is a faith in revelation, which is God's testimony. But revelation is claimed to come to men either through Scripture or by direct inspiration from God, and both these claims require examination by reason. For the variety of doctrines claimed as divine truth by the sects and their inconsistency with each other make it obvious that 'firmness of persuasion is no proof that any proposition is from God'.[13]

In the chapter on Enthusiasm, which does not appear in the first edition of the *Essay*, Locke queries the prevalent claims to revelation by direct inspiration.

Immediate revelation being a much easier way for men to establish their opinions and regulate their conduct than the tedious and not always successful labour of strict reasoning, it is no wonder that some have been very apt to pretend to revelation and to persuade themselves that they are under the peculiar guidance of heaven in their actions and opinions.[14]

Locke agrees that 'it cannot be denied that God can enlighten the understanding by a ray darted into the mind immediately from the fountain of light', but such are 'the odd opinions and extravagant actions enthusiasm has run men into' that all such claims must be scrutinized by reason or confirmed by revelation before they can be accepted as true. Locke points out that scrutiny of a claim to revealed truth does not mean a demand that the truth in question should be demonstrable by reason; for, except for the existence of God, no religious truths – not even the immortality of the soul – are so demonstrable. What we must ask is whether the revelation comes from God. But this means whether it is consistent with the truth revealed in the Scriptures.[15]

To this source of truth we now turn. Here too we have to admit that faith or belief is the most we can achieve. We have to ask whether the Scriptures are the word of God, and we also have to interpret what they say; and for both answers we must go to reason. But reason on such matters cannot provide certainty, but only probable conclusions. 'And therefore in those cases our assent can be rationally no higher than the evidence of its being a revelation. . . . If the evidence . . . be only on probable proofs, our assent can reach no higher than an assurance or diffidence arising from the more or less apparent probability of the proofs.'[16] Even when we have grounds for believing that a passage of Scripture is a revelation, interpretation is still needed.

> I read the revelation of the Holy Scripture with a full assurance that all it delivers is true: and though this be a submission to the writings of those inspired authors which I neither have nor can have for those of any other men: yet I use . . . the same way to interpret to myself the sense of that book that I do of any other. First I endeavour to understand the words and phrases of the language I read it in. . . . And if there be any word or expression which in that author, or in that place of that author, seems to have a peculiar meaning . . . that idea also I endeavour to form in my mind by comparing this author with himself and observing the design of his discourse.[17]

Locke therefore rejects any idea of a conflict between reason and faith or any subjection of one to the other. He sums up the matter effectively:

> Reason is natural revelation whereby the eternal Father of light and fountain of all knowledge communicates to mankind that portion of truth which he has laid within the reach of their natural faculties: revelation is natural reason enlarged by a new set of discoveries communicated by God immediately, which reason vouches the truth of by the testimony and proofs it gives that they come from God. So that he that takes away reason to make way for revelation puts out the light of both.[12]

Yet reason is supreme both as a source of absolute certainty and as the final court of appeal. If a truth is disclosed both by reason and by revelation, reason prevails since it provides knowledge, and revelation only probable belief.[19] If reason and a claim to revelation conflict then reason prevails and the claim has to be rejected. If we are asked to believe something which our reason rejects as impossible (e.g. that something should be in two places at the same time) we must reject the belief. For if we do not trust reason here we cannot trust her anywhere and this would make impossible the validation and interpretation of scriptural doctrines, and the difference between truth and falsehood would vanish.[20] On the other hand revelation can provide truths which unaided reason cannot; and if revelation indicates a doctrine which reason itself would deem improbable (miracles or the immortality of the soul might be examples) then revelation should be trusted.[21]

(iii) Christian Doctrine

At his own time Locke would have been accurately described as a latitudinarian. The rejection of dogmatic beliefs, resultant on the substitution of the Protestant principles of individual interpretation of scripture for the infallible authority of Rome, led Locke to an examination of Scripture with a view to establish which doctrines are essential to salvation. But the distinction between essential and unessential runs right through his life. As J. W. Gough has pointed out, a Latin essay of 1661 is entitled *Infallibilis Scripturæ Interpres non Necessarius*;[22] and, as will be indicated later, the early tracts on the powers of the magistrate rested on a distinction between essential and indifferent matters (see chapter 20, p. 172). But it was not until his last book published in his own lifetime that Locke set himself to work out what the essential doctrines were. In *The Reasonableness of Christianity* he argues, on the evidence of the Gospels, that the one belief both necessary and sufficient for salvation is the belief that Jesus is the Messiah, the son of God.[23] It might be argued that the Acts and the Epistles provide other doctrines necessary for salvation, and that less was required of believers at the dawn of Christianity than later authority revealed. This is met by the evidence of St John's Gospel which confirms the others in requiring only the one central belief, and which is later in date than the Acts and the Epistles.[24] The advantages of this limitation are obvious to Locke.

All the doctrines which might be added to it as necessary to salvation involve difficulty and arouse controversy (for example 'He descended into Hell'[25]). Different sects make different doctrines essential. (For example, again, the Athanasian creed begins 'Whosoever will be saved, before all things it is necessary that he hold the Catholic Faith . . . and the Catholic Faith is this: that we worship one God in Trinity and Trinity in Unity' – a doctrine expanded in the thirty difficult verses which follow.) If belief in every tenet to be found in the New Testament were made essential for salvation, the resulting creed would be of enormous length and extreme intellectual difficulty. That Jesus is the son of God is

> a plain intelligible proposition; and the all-merciful God seems here to have consulted the poor of this world and the bulk of mankind. These are articles that the labouring and illiterate man may comprehend. This is a religion suited to vulgar capacities, and the state of mankind in this world destined to labour and travel [sc. travail]. The writers and wranglers in religion fill it with niceties and dress it up with notions which they make necessary and fundamental parts of it; as if there were no way into the Church but through the Academy or the Lyceum. The greatest part of mankind have not leisure for learning and logic and superfine distinctions of the schools[26]

Locke does not dismiss as irrelevant or unimportant the other doctrines listed in the creeds or discoverable in the Scriptures. All of them are worthy of consideration and men should study the Scriptures and get the greatest help they can from them. But to make these doctrines essential to salvation is to overlook their origins and purpose. Most of them come from the Epistles. These were letters written on special occasions, and addressed to special audiences with special needs, and therefore cannot be regarded as stating doctrines essential to the salvation of all mankind. Their tenets are proper objects of faith and to be received as such, but they are not essential to salvation; and ignorance of any tenet from them does not condemn the ignorant to 'perish everlastingly'.[21]

It may be objected that the belief that Jesus is the son of God is not alone sufficient for salvation since the devils believe this too.[28] Lockes agrees that more is needed, but what is needed is not more beliefs. We require repentance and obedience to God's law.[29]

This law is itself to be found in the revelation of the Scriptures. Reason is an inadequate instrument for its discovery; and, even if it were adequate, the law would be revealed only to philosophers and theologians, to men capable of following intricate demonstrations of a mathematical type. For the mass of mankind, revelation is the surer and shorter way.[30] Obedience to God's law has also been made possible for Christians by the promise of the rewards available in an after-life (Cf. chapter 12, p. 127). It has been assisted too by the support of the Spirit in the battle against temptation.

Locke's language suggests that no one could be expected to follow God's commandments, with their demands for self-sacrifice, unless he were convinced that his happiness in an after-life depended on it. If so, the belief in immortality and its rewards and punishments would in fact be another belief essential to salvation, because essential to that obedience without which no one can be saved.

The publication of *The Reasonableness of Christianity* multiplied the doubts about Locke entertained by orthodox Christian theologians. Stillingfleet had already found in the *Essay* a rational basis for the anti-Trinitarian arguments which were then growing among Deists and Unitarians. He argues that belief in the Trinity requires clear and distinct ideas of 'nature' and 'person' and these are not attainable through sensation and reflection.[31] Locke therefore makes belief in the Trinity impossible. Locke replies that clear and distinct ideas are not essential for rational certainty; and that, even if the charge against him were proved, this would not show he was on one side of the Trinity–Unity controversy but that he was incapable of taking either side in it.[32]

In Stillingfleet's final letter he makes it clear that he is not accusing Locke directly of unorthodox religious views. His claim is now that Locke's philosophical theories can be used and had been used (by Toland, for example, as Toland stated) as a basis for Deistic conclusions.[33] While much of Stillingfleet's attack on Locke was well-aimed, as has been noted above, it did not touch theology.

But the apprehensions expressed by Stillingfleet were more than confirmed by the publication of *The Reasonableness of Christianity*. For here the doctrine of the Trinity is not counted as necessary for salvation, nor is the Atonement, nor the Virgin Birth, nor the Resurrection. Both during the remainder of Locke's lifetime and in the years immediately after his death, he was attacked as encouraging atheism, Unitarianism and Deism by these exclusions. To one attack, by John Edwards, Locke replied with a brief *Vindication*. When Edwards returned to the charge, Locke responded with a *Second Vindication* twice the length of the original work it defends. His defence is completely successful. He repeats that he is not denying doctrines which he does not regard as necessary for salvation. Indeed he believes in the Virgin Birth and the Resurrection and in miracles, though he does not believe in original sin nor in hell. He challenges his critic to tell him 'what those doctrines are which are absolutely necessary to be proposed to every man to make him a Christian', and then 'whether they are all the truths of divine revelation contained in the Bible'.[34] He then shows how Mr Edwards as 'arbiter and dispenser' selects his own set of doctrines as fundamental. This Locke finds typical of all systems 'set up by particular men or parties as the just measure of every man's faith'.[35]

Part Four
Political Theory

14 The Two Treatises

Locke's two *Treatises of Government*[1] were first published in 1689 but
were only admitted by Locke to be his own work in a codicil to his
will. This secrecy resulted in very inadequate revisions for later
editions and it was only with the sixth edition in 1764 that a text
approximating to Locke's intentions became available. Mr P.
Laslett has traced the complex history of the work and has provided a definitive text, including a collation with earlier editions.

He has also shown conclusively that the popular view that the
work was written after the Revolution of 1688 (and as a defence of
it) is true in only a minimal sense. Certainly there were last
minute additions and revisions to justify the dethronement of
James II. But there is much evidence that the main bulk of text
was written between 1679 and 1682, and that its criticisms
of monarchy are directed, in Shaftesbury's interest, against
Charles II.

The *First Treatise* was a refutation of the defence of absolute
monarchy by Sir Robert Filmer, a defence based on the dominion
given by God to Adam. This *Treatise*, written with great spirit and
vigour, though as usual at inordinate length, is an effective piece
of destructive argument. But it is now of purely historical interest
and need not concern us further.

The *Second Treatise* (specifically entitled *Of Civil Government*),
however, is one of the most influential works on political theory
ever written, ranking with the work of Rousseau and Marx.

15 The State of Nature

In the *Second Treatise* (on Civil Government), Locke makes his start from the notion of the state of nature, which is the condition of men living without political superiors. Locke regarded this state as the original condition of mankind (as will be noted in chapter 18), but he also treats it as the condition men would be in if there were no governments, and notes that independent states are, in relation to each other, in a state of nature, since there is no political superior over them all.

The state of nature is one of complete freedom. We shall see later that Locke has some misgivings about this; but freedom is described as being independent of the will of any other man;[1] and, if we interpret this as not being under the authority of another, the statement becomes a tautology, for this is what 'state of nature' means.

It is also a state of equality – equality in 'power and jurisdiction' since all men have 'the same advantage of nature and the use of the same faculties'.[2] Later Locke explains that, in saying that all men are by nature equal, he does not mean equality of every kind. Age or virtue, excellence or merit, birth, alliance or benefits may place one man above another. But they are equal in the sense that no one has dominion or jurisdiction over another.[3] This again is a tautology, for a 'state of nature' is defined as one in which men have no political superiors. To achieve consistency with the other quotations 'power' must be interpreted as equivalent to political authority, not as strength of body or dominating personality; and 'same faculties' must mean 'same in general though differing in degree'. All men have reason but 'there is a great variety in men's understandings'.[4]

142

There is an apparent limit on man's freedom in the state of nature; it operates 'within the bounds of the law of nature'.[5] This is ambiguous, and the ambiguity goes some way to explain Locke's contradictory accounts of the state of nature. It may mean that men are free to do whatever does not break the law of nature, or that they are free to do whatever they will; but they ought not to break the law of nature. It is an ambiguity natural to the term 'law of nature' which covers physical laws, which cannot be broken but only universally exemplified, and moral laws which can. The same contradiction appears neatly encapsulated in the lines of the hymn:

> Laws which never shall be broken
> For their guidance He hath made.

The law of nature lays down that 'no one ought to harm another in his life, health, liberty or possessions'.[6] Here the law is clearly a moral obligation, which may or may not be fulfilled in the exercise of human freedom. Yet it seems that a belief that the law would be universally operative is required to justify Locke's account of the state of nature as a state of 'peace, good will, mutual assistance and preservation'.[7] The problem posed by this description is that forcibly put, later in the *Second Treatise*, by Locke himself. 'If man in the state of nature be so free, as has been said; if he be absolute lord of his own person and possessions, equal to the greatest and subject to nobody, why will he part with his freedom? Why will he give up this empire and subject himself to the dominion and control of any other power?'[8] If the state of nature is so idyllic, why leave it? The truth is that the more Locke thought about the state of nature the worse it came to look.

The process begins at once with the recognition that there may be men who will break the laws of nature – 'offenders', 'transgressors'. Locke sometimes tries to maintain that even these offenders are trying to obey the law of nature as they see it. 'They who through passion or interest shall mis-cite or misapply it cannot so easily be convinced of their mistake where there is no established judge.'[9] But in general he has to admit that offenders break a law of whose existence they are well aware. For 'in transgressing the law of nature, the offender declares himself to live by another rule than that of reason and common equity, which

143

is the measure God has set to the actions of men, for their mutual security.'[10] It is admitted that the disobedience need not be conscious at the time of action; passion may blind a man to his obligations. 'For though the law of nature be plain and intelligible to all rational creatures; yet men being biassed by their interest, as well as ignorant for want of study of it, are not apt to allow of it as a law binding to them in the application of it to their particular cases.'[11]

When, in the state of nature, a man breaks the law of nature by damaging the interests of a fellow man, every man has a right to punish him; for someone ought to punish him in order to deter him and others from committing similar offences. And, since in that state all are equal in jurisdiction, if anyone has a right to punish all have a similar right.[12] In addition, the injured party has an individual right to reparation equivalent to the damage done to him.[13] There will be individual offenders and everyone is entitled to punish them. Why did Locke find such a state 'not to be endured'? The answer is that it has great 'inconveniences' resulting from men being judges in their own case so that 'ill-nature, passion and revenge will carry them too far in punishing others'.[14] Locke is here assuming that the injured party will impose the punishment, forgetting his distinction between the right to punish which is general and the right to reparation which belongs to the victim. It might be argued that the claim to reparation will be inflated by revenge, and also perhaps that the victim or his friends (who have an equal right with all others to impose punishment) would be the most likely to exercise the right to punish and to exercise it unfairly. The alternative is lynch law. But crowds are liable to waves of irrational emotion – and the absence of a 'machine' is the opening for the demagogue. And the process is unsatisfactory for dealing with crimes committed in secret, and requiring skill and organisation both for detection and arrest, and for unbiassed processes of justice. These, and not merely the 'inconveniences' of men being judges in their own case, are the arguments against society without government.

Government comes into existence, then, to provide an impartial authority to punish offences against the law of nature and to decide controversies between individual citizens. We have seen how this need arises from two distinct weaknesses in the state of nature, both of which involve a falling away from the idyllic condition of 'peace and good will' attributed to it: first, the anti-

144

social actions of offenders; and second, the biassed and irrational reactions of victims. If Locke stopped here, his attack on Hobbes might be justified. Some men, he says, have confounded the state of nature with the state of war, when they are 'as far distant as a state of peace, good will, mutual assistance and preservation and a state of enmity, malice, violence and mutual destruction are from one another'.[15] Laslett defends Locke here by insisting that, although war is not absent from the state of nature, it is an 'incident' not a 'condition'.[16] But this is to forget that Hobbes distinguishes between *war* (which to him is a *condition* of fear and insecurity) and *battle* (which is the 'incident' when the insecurity erupts in conflict). Bad weather does not mean continuous rain, but unreliable weather with a tendency to occasional rain.[17] Nevertheless, so far as we have gone, Locke's picture suggests a state in which most men live together in peace and good will and obey the law of nature, offenders being the exception and the need to discipline them only an occasional incident. This would indeed be different from Hobbes' picture.

But Locke recurred time and again to the state of nature and his view of it became continuously more gloomy. His answer to the question 'why should men leave the state of nature?' becomes:

> . . . it is obvious that, though in the state of nature he hath such a right, yet the enjoyment of it is very uncertain, and constantly exposed to the invasion of others. For all being kings as much as he . . . and the greater part no strict observers of equity and justice, the enjoyment of the property he has in this state is very unsafe, very insecure. This makes him willing to quit this condition which, however free, is full of fears and continual dangers.[18]

> Thus mankind, notwithstanding all the privileges of the state of nature, being put in a ill condition while they remain in it, are quickly driven into society.[19]

'Full of fears and continual dangers' is exactly Hobbes's description of the state of nature; and the offenders are now not an insignificant minority but 'the greater part' which are 'no strict observers of equity and justice'. Locke goes one further in the first *Letter on Toleration*.

> The pravity of mankind being such that they had rather injuriously prey on the fruits of other mens labour's than take

pains to provide for themselves, the necessity of preserving men in the possession of what honest industry has already acquired and also of preserving their liberty and strength whereby they may acquire what they farther want, obliges men to enter into society with one another.[20]

The 'greater part' now gives way to 'mankind'. There seems now no doubt that Locke's state of nature, far from being one of 'peace, goodwill, mutual assistance and preservation', would be as intolerable as Hobbes painted it, and Locke's justification for government – the overwhelming need for security and an ending of the state of war (which is identical with the state of nature) – is the same as that of Hobbes.

Yet there are two differences between Locke and Hobbes. Locke's men in the state of nature have moral obligations, of which, if they will listen to reason, they become aware; and correspondingly they have natural rights. Both of these, the duties and the rights, carry over into society and are not the result of it. Except for a few inconsistent lapses, Hobbes allows his natural man no moral standards and no rights. But, as we have seen, this makes little difference to the state of nature. For Locke, most men fail to live up to their moral standards; and it is an open question whether one would wish to live among a lot of amoral men or a lot of immoral men. The other great difference between Locke and Hobbes is that, for Hobbes, the one fatal flaw in the state of nature is the threat to *life*. All other ills flow naturally from it. For Locke, the main emphasis is on the threat to *property*: and it is to provide security for property that the civil society is founded. This is Locke's unique contribution to political theory.

16 Property

Locke derives the right to private property from the right of self-preservation. God gave the earth to mankind for its use; and this means to men in general not to specific individuals. But, if a man is to live, he must be able to appropriate natural objects for food and drink. He must be able to 'remove' them from the common stock, to 'gather' them, for his own use. This right requires no consent from other men; if it did the man would starve.[1] But, besides this right to appropriate things for his own immediate use and sustenance, a man can also make something his own property by 'mixing his labour' with the raw materials nature provides. He may till, plant, improve, cultivate a piece of land; and, because his labour has altered it, it becomes his property.

So we come to the 'labour theory of value'. There are traces of this in some of Locke's contemporaries, but he first made it the centre of a systematic defence of property. He argues that, if one considers the value of the products of the earth, nine tenths or ninety nine hundredths or even nine hundred and ninety nine thousandths will be found to be attributable to labour and only the remaining fraction to nature itself.[2] A man's labour and the work of his hands are necessarily his own and so also should be their products. To say that anything is a man's property is to say that he can do what he likes with it including making gifts of it, and, it should follow, bequeathing it to whomever he likes at his own death.

There are three questions which arise from this theory. The first is whether the right of acquisition by labour is unlimited. Locke appears to impose a limit when he says a man may appropriate as much as he can use. If he appropriates more, it will spoil and go to waste and this is not permissible.[3] But the limitation can be evaded by the use of money. If surplus products which would spoil if hoarded are exchanged for money, which cannot spoil if hoarded, then there need be no limit to the process of acquisition.[4]

Secondly, there is an internal inconsistency in the labour theory of property. For a man who receives a gift[5] or legacy[6] will have property for which he has done no work and to which he would therefore seem to have no claim. (The differential treatment of 'unearned income' and steep death duties are indications of a similar contradiction and the compromises to which it leads.) Moreover, the freedom to dispose or settle one's estate as one pleases[7] denies the right of children to inherit, and brings into conflict the right of property and the rights of wife and children, which Locke admits when he says a conqueror who has a right to kill his defeated enemy has no right to take the goods of his wife and children; 'they too had a title to the goods he enjoyed and their shares in the estate he possessed'.[8] (Again the compromises between these two claims in the laws of inheritance in various countries show the practical interest of this problem.)

But the notion of unearned income has a much more striking and obvious application, and that is the position of hired labour. Locke seems to have been unaware of this difficulty. In a notorious passage he writes: 'Thus the grass my horse has bit, the turfs my servant has cut and the ore I have digged in any place where I have a right to them in common with others become my property without the assignation or consent of anybody. The labour that was mine removing them out of that common state they were in hath fixed my property in them.'[9] Locke, if asked how it was that his servant's labour should count as his and why the turfs should not belong to the servant, would no doubt reply that he had worked for the money which enabled him to hire the servant, and that the servant's labour is his own property and he can therefore do what he likes with it; and this includes 'alienating' it. But the contradiction remains:

For 'tis not barely the ploughman's pains, the reaper's and thresher's toil and the baker's sweat is to be counted into the bread we eat; the labour of those who broke the oxen, who digged and wrought the iron and stones, who felled and framed the timber, employed about the plough, mill, oven or any

148

other utensils, which are a vast number requisite to this corn, from its being seed to be sown to its being made bread, must all be charged on the account of labour.[10]

Even in Locke's day much of the labour thus listed must have been hired labour. The conflict is here between the labour theory of property and the principle of liberty. For the latter would require that a man may alienate his labour by contract, as he can alienate his property by gift or legacy. The contradictions involved are similar to those involved in the right of a free man to sell himself into slavery or that of a free citizen to work for the destruction of political liberty. 'A free man makes himself a servant of another by selling him for a certain time the service he undertakes to do in exchange for certain wages he is to receive'.[11]

It may be argued that, when all available common land has been enclosed, a man who has none has no choice but to make himself a hired labourer. This is not so, however, as the examples cited above show. At any stage in the productive process a man may improve the results of another man's labour, paying the other man the value of the labour already contributed. Thus, according to the labour theory of value, the miller and the baker need not own land in order to benefit. Yet there may be men who have not the resources for any 'self-employed' activity and who therefore necessarily fall into the hired servant class. Locke would be inclined to believe that men are poor by their own fault through lack of industry; and thus in the last resort this is their choice.

Locke's only defence of the position of the hired labourer is the argument that the unlimited acquisition of property, because of the immense increase in production which it involves, provides even the poorest labourer with a standard of living higher than that enjoyed by a 'King in America', where there is no enclosure or tillage.[12] 'For I ask whether in the wild woods and uncultivated waste of America left to nature without any improvement, tillage, or husbandry, a thousand acres will yield the needy and wretched inhabitants as many conveniences of life as ten acres of equally fertile land do in Devonshire where they are well cultivated?' Thus 'he who appropriates land to himself by his own labour does not lessen but increase the common stock of mankind'.[13]

The third question arising from Locke's theory of property relates to the basic difference we noted (p. 146 above) between Hobbes and Locke regarding the function of government. The sole function of government for Hobbes is the preservation of life, whereas for Locke political power is defined as 'a right of making laws with penalties of death and consequently all less penalties for the regulating and preserving of property and of employing the force of the community in the execution of such laws and in defence of the commonwealth from foreign injury and all this only for the public good'.[14] Did Locke mean then that government had no duty to protect life? The answer is, as so often, that Locke is ambiguous and inconsistent. He sometimes uses 'property' in a wide sense so as to include life and indeed other goods, as well as material possessions. When men leave the state of nature because they find it a state 'full of fears and continual dangers' they join others to 'unite for the mutual preservation of their lives, liberties, and estates, which I call by the general name property'.[15] So too, in the *First Letter Concerning Toleration*, he says:

the commonwealth seems to me to be a society of men constituted only for the procuring, preserving and advancing of their own civil interests. Civil interest I call life, liberty, health, and indolency of body; and the possession of outward things such as money, lands, houses, furniture, and the like. It is the duty of the civil magistrate by the impartial execution of equal laws to secure unto all people in general and to every one of his subjects in particular the just possession of these things belonging to this life. If anyone presume to violate the laws of public justice and equity established for the preservation of these things, his presumption is to be checked by the fear of punishment, consisting in the deprivation or diminution of those civil interests or goods which otherwise he might and ought to enjoy. But seeing no man does willingly suffer himself to be punished by the deprivation of any part of his goods, and much less of his liberty or life, therefore is the magistrate armed with the force and strength of all his subjects in order to the punishment of those that violate any other man's rights.[16]

17 The Foundation of Government

(*i*) *A Historical Event.* It was the view of Locke that government emerged in history from a pre-existing state of nature. 'That which begins and actually constitutes any political society is nothing but the consent of any number of freemen capable of a majority to unite and incorporate into such a society. And this is that and that only which could give beginning to any lawful government in the world.'[1] It may be objected, says Locke, that there is no record of any such historical beginning. The reply is that this is not surprising because government is everywhere antecedent to records.[2] Rome and Venice were in fact founded by just such voluntary agreements. And, if it is said that the state of nature nowhere existed but all men are born under government, Joseph Acosta may be quoted as maintaining 'that in many parts of America there was no government at all'.[3] 'In the beginning', Locke observes 'all the world was America.'[4]

(*ii*) *Society and Government.* In most of his references to the foundation of government Locke describes the process as a move by which men leave the state of nature by giving up their right of punishment and redress to a government. But in chapter XIX "Of the Dissolution of Government", we are suddenly introduced to a two-stage process: the creation of a political society, and then the appointment of a government. The object of this is to argue that government can be dissolved without the dissolution of society (an argument relevant to the defence of revolution which Locke is undertaking). 'That which makes the community and brings men out of the loose state of nature into one political society is the agreement which everyone has with the rest to incorporate and act as one body and so be one distinct commonwealth.'[5]

Here, in the distinction between society and government, may be found traces in Locke of the view that man is naturally social, independently of law and authority. 'God having made man such a creature that in his own judgement it was not good for him to be alone, put him under strong obligations of necessity, convenience and inclination to drive him into society, as well as fitted him with understanding and language to continue and enjoy it. The first society was between man and wife, which gave beginning to that between parents and children, to which in time that between master and servant came to be added.'[6] Besides these bonds, there are all those relationships of friendship and of economic interchange which bind men independently of government. All this indeed might seem to bring us back to that conception of the idyllic state of nature as one of 'peace, good will, mutual assistance and preservation'. The dissolution of *government* then would leave *society* intact.

But this account of Locke cannot be sustained. He himself repeatedly rejects the view that the creation of a *political* society is an act independent of and logically preceding the appointment of a government. The disappearance of government would result not in a condition of social unity but in a return to the intolerable conditions of the state of nature. 'To avoid this state of war (wherein is no appeal but to heaven and wherein every least difference is apt to end where there is no authority to decide between the contenders) is one great reason of men's putting themselves into society and quitting the state of nature. For where there is an authority, a power on earth, from which relief can be had by appeal, there the continuance of the state of war is excluded and the controversy decided by that power.'[7]

Because no political society can be nor subsist without having in itself the power to preserve the property and, in order thereunto, to punish the offences of all those of that society, there and there only is political society where every one of the members hath quitted this natural power, resigned it up into the hands of the community in all cases that exclude him not from appealing for protection to the law established by it . . . whereby it is easy to discern who are and who are not in political society together. Those who are united into one body and have a common established law and judicature to appeal to, with authority to decide controversies between them and punish offenders are in civil society one with another; but those who have no such common appeal, I mean on earth, are still in the state of nature, each being, where there is no other, judge for himself and executioner, which is, as I have before showed it, the perfect state of nature.[8]

'Wherever any number of men are so united into one society as to quit every one his executive power of the law of nature and to resign it to the public, there and there only is a political or civil society. . . . And this is done wherever any number of men in the state of nature enter into society to make one people, one body politic under one supreme government.'[9] In the paragraph immediately following that which emphasises the distinction between the dissolution of government and the dissolution of society, Locke writes:

Governments are dissolved from within, first, when the legislative is altered. Civil society being a state of peace, amongst those who are of it, from whom the state of war is excluded by the umpirage which they have provided in their legislative for the ending all differences that may arise amongst any of them, 'tis in their legislative that the members of a commonwealth are united and combined together into one coherent living body. This is the soul that gives form life and unity to the commonwealth . . . and therefore when the legislative is broken or dissolved, dissolution and death follow.[10]

James II, it is implied, put himself into a state of war with his people, dissolved the government, and left them 'to that defence which belongs to every one in the state of nature'.[11]

There is one more way by which government may be dissolved and that is when he who has the supreme executive power neglects and abandons that charge, so that the laws already made can no longer be put in execution. This is demonstratively to reduce all to anarchy and so effectually to dissolve the government . . . the government visibly ceases and the people become a confused multitude without order or connexion.[12]

For if anyone by force takes away the established legislative of any society and the laws by them made pursuant to their trust, he thereby takes away the umpirage which everyone had consented to for a peaceable decision of all their controversies and a bar to the state of war among them.[13]

It is clear why Locke wishes to have it both ways – both to maintain that a civil society is not dissolved when its government is destroyed, and also to insist that the dissolution of the government does dissolve the society and produce a state or war (a return to the state of nature). He wishes to use the Hobbistic threats of anarchy and chaos to justify government. But he wishes also to maintain that when governments have been attacked and the legislative has been crippled, the same people whose government has been destroyed have a right to oust the tyrant and set up a new government. Thus the community must remain in existence and capable of united action throughout. This he achieves in one place by invoking direct majority rule.

The only way whereby anyone divests himself of his natural liberty and puts on the bonds of civil society is by agreeing with other men to join and unite into a community for their comfortable, safe and peaceable living one amongst another in a secure enjoyment of their properties and a greater security against any that are not of it. . . . When any number of men have so consented to make one community or government they are thereby presently incorporated and make one body politic, wherein the majority have a right to act and conclude the rest. For when any number of men have by the consent of every individual made a community they have thereby made that community one body with a power to act as one body, which is only by the will and determination of the majority. For that which acts [sc. activates] any community being only the consent of the individuals of it and it being necessary to that which is one body to move one way, it is necessary the body should move that way whither the greater force carries it, which is the consent of the majority: or else it is impossible it should act or continue one body, one community, which the consent of every individual that united into it agreed that it should; and so everyone is bound by that consent to be concluded by the majority. . . . And thus every man, by consenting with others to make one body politic under one government puts himself under an obligation to everyone of that society to

154

submit to the determination of the majority and be concluded by it; or else his original compact whereby he with others incorporates into one society would signify nothing and be no compact if he be left free and under no other ties than he was before in the state of nature.[14]

The argument here is: (*a*) uniting with others into one body is meaningless unless that body can act, and it can act only by majority decision; (*b*) such uniting is meaningless if it involves no 'ties' or obligations other than those of the state of nature. But the only source of obligation in a voluntary society is majority decision. But this means once again that it is impossible to separate the creation of society from the creation of government. Nevertheless it is true that, when a government is dissolved, the society whose government it is is not dissolved but is able to create a new government. What Locke must argue, however, is that it is not only able but immediately obliged to create a new government; for the condition of anarchy will rapidly become one of chaos and fear in the absence of any constituted authority. Law-abiding habits and mutual trust and co-operation will not long survive the disappearance of governmental power.

Social Relations Independent of Civil Society

So far we have been considering the view that the formation of a civil society takes place in two stages, the unification into a society and the establishment of a government, and maintaining that most of Locke's arguments make such a distinction impossible. There is, however, another sense in which 'society precedes government', and where Locke is consistent and certainly right.

As we noted above (p. 152), he held that man was naturally a social being and the first society was the family, including parents, children and servants. There is also all the infinite variety of social relationships which arise and continue independently of civil governments. There are the voluntary associations, of which churches are the most important for Locke, which are also independent of government. Thus the state of nature is social though not political. 'Wherever there are any number of men, *however associated*, that have no decisive power to appeal to, there they are still in the state of nature.'[15] [My italics.] The danger here is to speak as if these social relations constituted *a society*. The only *single society* to which these considerations would lead would be that consisting of all mankind. Locke moves in this direction when he considers the obligations which men have independently of government and state law. In the state of nature man has a power 'to do whatsoever he thinks fit for the preservation of himself and others within the permission of the law of nature: by which law common to them all he and the rest of mankind are one community, make up one society distinct from all other creatures. And were it not for the corruption and viciousness of degenerate men there would be no need of any other; no necessity that men should separate from this great and natural community and by positive agreements combine into smaller and divided associations.'[16]

The only passages which can be interpreted as describing societies without government are those which refer to tribal life in America. Though, in most cases, Locke speaks of these tribes as having 'kings' or 'rulers',[17] he quotes Joseph Acosta on the Peruvians: 'There are great and apparent conjectures, says he, that these men for a long time had neither kings nor commonwealth but lived in troops, as they do to this day in Florida, the Cheriquanas, those of Brazil and many other nations, which have no certain kings, but as occasion is offered in peace or war, they choose their captains as they please.'[18]

18 The Justification of Government

(*i*) *Protection*. Government comes into existence in order to protect property, whether in the narrow sense of possessions, or widened to include life, health and liberty. Thus it would seem that any actions of government or any powers attributed to it must be justified by their contribution to this end. Hobbes had argued in this way from his narrower premiss, the protection of life. From such premisses nothing necessarily follows concerning the form of government. 'The sovereign, be he a man or an assembly of men', says Hobbes; though he goes on to argue that monarchy is most likely to achieve that security which is the end of government. Locke argues, in the reverse direction, that absolute monarchy is the greatest possible danger to those rights which government exists to protect.

> As if when men quitting the state of nature entered into society they agreed that all of them but one should be under the restraint of laws but that he should still retain all the liberty of the state of nature increased with power and made licentious by impunity. This is to think that men are so foolish that they take care to avoid what mischiefs may be done them by polecats or foxes, but are content, nay think it safety, to be devoured by lions.[1]

Moreover, as will be shown later (p. 169), the right of revolution by the people against any government rests entirely on the concept of breach of trust and the trust is the preservation of property.

Here then is Locke's basic answer to the problem of political obligation. Government is justified when it does (and unjustified

157

when it does not) protect property. It should follow (as it does in Hobbes) that the structure of government and its constitution should be determined by this function, by the answer to the question 'What constitution and what forms of government will be most likely to protect property?'. But a different answer appears when Locke considers how governments are founded.

(*ii*) *Consent.* As we have seen (p. 154), Locke maintains that uniting into a single community obliges its members to be bound by majority decisions, because action requires consent. But the move from consent to majority decision in the passage in question is covered merely by an analogy with physical forces. 'It being necessary to that which is one body to move one way, it is necessary the body should move that way whither the greater force carries it, which is the consent of the majority.'[2] Locke's problem is the same as that of Rousseau. 'Why should majority decisions be taken as expressing the general will?'[3] This is especially difficult for Rousseau after his distinction between the 'general will' and the 'will of all'.[4] The general will is defined in terms of the common interest which even a unanimous vote need not necessarily express. Rousseau would seem compelled to take the line that majority decisions are necessarily in the common interest and this he does when he says that if, I find myself in the minority when the vote is taken, this shows that I was mistaken (about what the general will was).[5] The parallel would be for Locke to maintain that majority decisions necessarily achieve protection of property, the aim of government. But Rousseau has another answer. It was part of the original social contract (which was a unanimous decision) that on all future occasions majority decisions should be taken as expressing the general will.[6]

Both in Locke and in Rousseau this solution is stated in terms of an 'original' historical event. But the point may be made without this mythology. If there is to be 'consent', a democratic basis for government, this must involve participation by all in the process of decision-making. If this participation is to be expressed, it must be by individual votes. In that case a *constitutional* decision is required as to how the votes should be treated. The first option is that they should be advisory, and the decision should remain with a man or body of men not constitutionally required to be determined by them. If, however, the votes are to determine the decision there are three possibilities open. First, (and apparently the most democratic, since it assures that all voters are satisfied), would be the *unanimity* rule, that no decisions should be taken unless they are unanimous. But this is to make it likely that no decisions at all are taken because (as in the Security Council of the United Nations) one hostile vote can veto any action. The second possibility is that *minority* decisions should be taken as decisive. This would enable one recalcitrant not only to block action but to carry the decision. The third mode of making decisions is by *majority* voting. It is obvious then that, if decisions are to be taken by voting, the majority principle is the only one which *both* enables all to share the process *and* enables decisions to be made. This principle is unanimously accepted prior to any actual voting (as Rousseau said) in the sense that, unless it is understood as agreed, no democratic decision-making is possible.

Having thus the right to make decisions, binding on its own members, by majority vote, a political society may use this right either to make rules by majority votes or to delegate this power of legislation to a man or a selected group of men either for life or for some limited time.[7]

(*iii*) *Representative Government.* Locke has no hesitation in accepting the principle of delegated decision-making, and he seems to think no argument is needed. Sometimes he hardly seems aware of any distinction between direct and representative democracy. Whenever a man joins others to make a civil society, 'he authorises the society, or which is all one the legislature thereof, to make laws for him.'[8] 'Every single person became subject to those laws which he himself, *as part of the legislature*, had established'.[9] [My italics.] The legislature is the basic authority in the state.[10] This is because the making of laws has logical priority over the action of the executive in putting them into effect or of the judiciary in deciding cases which come under them.

Locke agrees that 'in the beginning' – that is, in primitive societies – it was natural that the power of law-making should be given to one outstanding man. But the dangers of absolute monarchy become in course of time so obvious that civilised peoples move on to the institution of an elected parliament.

Though perhaps at first some one good and excellent man, having got a pre-eminence amongst the rest, had this deference paid to his goodness and virtue, as to a kind of natural authority, that the chief rule, by a tacit consent, devolved into his hands, without any other caution, but the assurance they had of his uprightness and wisdom: yet when time . . . had brought in successors of another stamp the people finding their properties not secure under the government as then it was (whereas government has no other end but the preservation of property) could never be safe nor at rest nor think themselves in civil society until the legislature was placed in collective bodies of men, call them Senate, Parliament, or what you please.[11]

Tacit Consent

All the passages we have considered so far have referred to the historical foundation of the state and have based the claim to obedience from the citizens on the fact that they themselves either voted on the making of laws or elected the representatives who made them.[12] But Locke has to explain why the citizens of any actual state who were not present in person at its foundation are required to obey its laws. The answer is tacit consent. 'The consent of freemen, born under government, which only makes them members of it, being given separately in their turns, as each comes of age, and not in a multitude together, people take no notice of it, and thinking it not done at all, or not necessary, conclude they are naturally subjects as they are men.'[13] Locke sees that it is unlikely that such tacit consent would be generally thought to be a concomitant of coming of age; and also that it would at once be asked whether every inhabitant of a country gives consent at the age of twenty-one or eighteen. Locke's answer is that consent is a corollary of land-ownership.

It has been commonly supposed that a father could oblige his posterity to that government of which he himself was a subject, and that his compact held them: whereas it being only a necessary condition annexed to the land and the inheritance of an estate which is under that government, reaches only to those who will take it on that condition, and so is no natural tie or engagement but a voluntary submission.[14]

The son cannot ordinarily enjoy the possessions of his father, but under the same terms as his father did; by becoming a member of the society, whereby he puts himself presently under the government he finds there established, as much as any other subject of that commonwealth.[15]

Since the government has a direct jurisdiction only over the land, and reaches the possessor of it (before he has actually incorporated himself in the society) only as he dwells upon and enjoys that, the obligation anyone is under by virtue of such enjoyment begins and ends with the enjoyment; so that, wherever the owner who has given nothing but a tacit consent to the government will by donation, sale, or otherwise quit the said possession, he is at liberty to go and incorporate himself into any other commonwealth.[16]

Captives taken in a just war may be enslaved and 'being in the state of slavery, *not capable of any property,* cannot in that state be considered as any part of Civil Society'.[11] [My italics.] It seems in these passages that Locke is using property in the narrow sense as meaning possessions, or in an even narrower sense as equivalent to 'estates' or land.

If 'property' had been intended in the wide sense, then every inhabitant who enjoyed life, liberty or health would be understood to have given tacit consent to the acts of government and to be capable of full membership of civil society. And a hired labourer who owns his own tools or his apron could be said to have property whose protection he owes to the state, to which therefore he consents to give obedience. Locke is neither clear nor consistent on this crucial issue.

But submitting to the laws of any country, living quietly and enjoying privileges and protection under them, makes not a man a member of that society. This is only a local protection and homage due to and from all those who, not being in a state of war, come within the territories belonging to any government, to all parts whereof the force of its law extends. But this no more makes a man a member of that society, a perpetual subject of that commonwealth, than it would make a man a subject to another in whose family he found it convenient to abide for some time; though whilst he continued in it, he were obliged to comply with the laws and submit to the government he found there. And thus we see that foreigners, by living all their lives under another government and enjoying the privileges and protection of it, though they are bound, even in conscience, to submit to its administration as far forth as any denizen; yet do they not thereby come to be subjects or members of that commonwealth. Nothing can make a man so but the actually entering into it by positive engagement and express promise and compact. This is that, which I think, concerning the beginning of political societies and that consent which makes anyone a member of any commonwealth.[18]

Locke in this last sentence seems to have forgotten the qualification of tacit consent. And tacit consent, as we have seen, must be assumed to be given by those who enjoy the privilege of protection of property. His illustration of resident aliens in a modern state fails because the qualifications for citizenship (birth or parentage) which it implies are qualifications which he rejects. There is one passage which begins with the narrow sense of property but at the end (in the clause italicised below) seems to widen the qualification in such a way as certainly to include resident aliens.

> Nobody doubts but an express consent of any man entering into any society makes him a perfect member of that society. . . . The difficulty is, what ought to be looked upon as a tacit consent and how far it binds; i.e. how far anyone shall be looked on to have consented, and thereby submitted to any government, where he has made no expressions of it at all. And to this I say that any man that hath any possessions or enjoyment of any part of the dominion of any government doth thereby give his tacit consent and is so far forth obliged to obedience to the laws of that government during such enjoyment as anyone under it; whether this his possession be of land to him and his heirs for ever, *or a lodging only for a week; or whether it be barely travelling freely on the highway; and in effect it reaches as far as the very being of anyone within the territories of that government.*[19] [My italics.]

If express consent makes a man a 'full member' of society and nothing else can do so, then no society after the deaths of its founder members will have any full members at all. Hence tacit consent is necessary. But if tacit consent suffices, those who are assumed to give it are those who enjoy or possess any part of the dominion of a state, including anyone within the territories of the government, since they all enjoy life and liberty and personal possessions, if not landed estates.

It seems that Locke is confused and inconsistent here because he has the natural outlook of his time. The hired labourers lived in a kind of limbo in which they were sometimes remembered and

162

sometimes forgotten but never explicitly 'placed' in society. There are obvious parallels to this. The 'third class' in Plato's ideal state presents a number of problems which are unanswerable because Plato's social position and his consequent assumptions blinded him to their existence. Similarly Locke's chapter VI is headed "Paternal Power". He points out that all the arguments (and the scriptural references) give the father and mother equal status and that the power should therefore be more properly called 'parental' than 'paternal'.[20] But he frequently refers to the father as the sole authority in the family.[21] Again, this is natural because of the ambiguous social position of women, a position which could not be clearly defined nor effectively justified. So with the 'working class' in seventeenth–century England.

There are two possible lines to take. One is that members of the working class are not members of society (as slaves are not) and that the state as such has no concern with their welfare or rights (except to see that they do not disturb the peace). They should have no voice in its deliberations and be exempt from demands by the state on their wages or labour. The state would be the instrument for the protection of the property of the landowning class. (This is the view attributed to Locke by C. B. Macpherson in *The Political Theory of Possessive Individualism*). The other view would make all adults (? males) full citizens and the protection of their lives, liberties, health and possessions (not land only) the function of government. Universal (male ?) suffrage would be the corollary of this along with a (possibly graduated) system of taxation from which wages would not necessarily be exempt. Locke held neither position, and at his time this is no matter for surprise. His social assumptions would be shared by his readers. They could not see, as we can, how Locke's *arguments* are moving towards Rousseau and Tom Paine and Karl Marx.

The second basis suggested by Locke for obedience to government is therefore consent, and it is taken to authorise all majority decisions. What is to happen if the first and second bases conflict? A majority decision may well interfere with the property, or with the life, health, liberty or possessions of minority groups or individuals. A breach of trust justifies revolution against governments which fail to fulfil their protective function. But revolutions involve the return of power to the people; and the issue remains obscure if the people themselves fail in their protective function.

In connection with breach of trust, and in several other places, a wider justification for government than the negative one of protection seems to be suggested by Locke. The power reposed in the legislature shall be disposed 'as the good of the society shall require'; and the employment of the force of the community is to be 'directed to no other end but the peace, safety and public good of the people'.[22] The legislative power is 'limited to the public good of the society'.[23] 'The power the government has, being only for the good of the society. . . .'[24] Again, when the legislature is ineffective either because unforeseen or individual cases make laws inapplicable or because of flaws in its own constitution (rotten boroughs etc.), the power of prerogative may be used by the executive or the 'prince' to take the necessary action and the criterion for such action is, once again, the common good.

> *Salus populi suprema lex* is certainly so just and fundamental a rule that he who sincerely follows it cannot dangerously err . . . Prerogative being nothing but a power in the hands of the prince to provide for the public good. . . . Whatsoever cannot but be acknowledged to be of advantage to the society and people in general upon just and lasting measures, will always when done justify itself.[25]

'The good of the people' must be resolved into the good of individual members of society, and this criterion would seem to justify any legislation or executive action which would benefit the individuals conerned. But this overrides the essential distinction between protection – the benefits of security from damage by other people – and the control or assistance of an individual for his own good. This distinction formed the basis of J. S. Mill's political theory: other-regarding actions are liable to government interference, self-regarding actions, even if they are to the detriment of the agent, should be left alone. An example would be that of 'public health'. On Mill's principles infectious diseases could be compulsorily controlled, but otherwise an individual's health is his own affair. He should be free to consult a doctor if he wishes, to obey the doctor's 'orders' if he is so inclined, to enter hospital and to discharge himself from it at his own free will. But there are cases which cross this crucial frontier: drugs legislation, the proposed addition of fluoride to water supplies to preserve the teeth.

How would Locke stand on this issue? No consistent answer is to be found in him. In general his objective is protection, and at his time the notion of positive beneficial legislation was unfamiliar. Moreover most of the passages quoted above refer to the protective function in the same context as the 'common good'. And, on prerogative, the power is to be 'employed for the benefit of the community and suitably to the trust and ends of government'[26] – and the ends of government are regularly defined as the protection of property. There are, I believe, only two specific passages where the issue is clearly faced and they contradict each other. In his writings on Toleration, the issue seemed to Locke to be whether the government was entitled to control a man's religion for his own good. And in one place, in the *First Letter Concerning Toleration*, Locke widens his defence of toleration to the general principle that the government is not entitled to do anything to a man for his own good.

> In private domestic affairs, in the management of estates, in the conservation of bodily health, every man may consider what suits his own conveniency and follow what course he likes best. No man complains of the ill-management of his neighbour's affairs. No man is angry with another for an error committed in sowing his land, or in marrying his daughter. Nobody corrects a spendthrift for consuming his substance in taverns.[27]

In opposition to this is the passage in the *Second Treatise* where Locke gives a new and idealist twist to the meaning of 'liberty'.

> For law in its true notion is not so much the limitation as the direction of a free and intelligent agent to his proper interest and prescribes no further than is for the general good of those under that law. Could they be happier without it the law as a useless thing would of itself vanish; and that ill deserves the name of confinement which hedges us in only from bogs and precipices. So that, however it be mistaken, the end of law is not to abolish or restrain but to preserve and enlarge freedom.[28]

The language here, and the illustrations, are incompatible with the interpretation of law as the defence of individuals from damage by other people. Yet Locke seems unaware of the obvious implications, for the passage continues: 'For, in all the states of created

165

beings capable of laws, where there is no law there is no freedom. For liberty is to be free from restraint and violence from others which cannot be where there is no law.'

It cannot be denied that the whole general impression left by Locke's work is that the limitation of government action to the protection of individuals from damage by others was his basic theory. Nor is this surprising at his time and in the historical conditions under which he wrote. 'Poor relief' was the only official exception to this principle in the actual practice of governments. The great developments in health, education, and social security and welfare still lay in the distant future.

19 The Right of Revolution

When Locke says that there can be no constitutional solution to a conflict between the prince and the people (or between the executive and the legislature) about which of them is acting for the common good, he regularly adds that in such cases there is an appeal to heaven. This he interprets as equivalent to a right of the people to decide the issue by force.

Frequently throughout the *Second Treatise* Locke has urged that, if governments act unjustly, their subjects are back in the state of nature and therefore have a right to use force against the injustice.

> Force without right upon a man's person makes a state of war, both where there is and where there is not a common judge.[1]

> Where an appeal to the law and constituted judges lies open, but the remedy is denied by a manifest perverting of justice and a barefaced wresting of the laws to protect or indemnify the violence or injuries of some men or party of men, there it is hard to imagine anything but a state of war.[2]

This comes from a passage added in 1689 and therefore directly referring to the Revolution of 1688.[3]

What now becomes clear in the later stages of his argument is that the people must be the judge of whether the public good has been endangered and their view has a right to prevail.

> Though the people cannot be judge so as to have by the constitution of that society any superior power to determine and give effective sentence in the case; yet they have by a law antecedent and paramount to all positive laws of men reserved that ultimate determination to themselves which belongs to all

167

mankind where there lies no appeal on earth, *viz.* to judge whether they have just cause to make their appeal to heaven, and this judgment they cannot part with, it being out of a man's power so to submit himself to another as to give him a liberty to destroy him.[4]

The conditions under which this right may come to the people are discussed in some detail in chapter xix "Of the Dissolution of Government". This may occur: 1. when unauthorised people arrogate to themselves the right to make laws; 2. when a prince substitutes his arbitrary will for the laws previously properly enacted; 3. when the prince interferes with the functioning of the legislature: 4. when the elections or methods of election of representatives are altered without the consent and against the interests of the people; 5. where the people are delivered into the hands of a foreign power either by the prince or by the legislature; and, 6. when the executive fails or refuses to put the laws into execution.[5] In all these cases the prince (or the executive) is said to be responsible for the dissolution, because only the prince has the power to commit these abuses without open revolution by abuse of his prerogative. Locke also points out that these events are best described not as victories of the prince over the legislature but as the destruction of the old legislature and the creation of a new one, since the legislature in any society is that body with the *actual* authority to issue laws.

The result in all cases of such dissolution is that 'the people are at liberty to provide for themselves, by erecting a new legislative, differing from the other [sc. the usurping legislative] by the change of persons or form or both as they shall find it most for their safety and good'.[6]

Besides the six ways enumerated above by which a government may be dissolved – all of them involving interference with the legislative and abuses of executive power – there is another and quite different case for revolution: when the legislative acts against the trust reposed in them, namely to protect the lives, liberties and fortunes of the people.[7] Locke's language in this context suggests that society would be dissolved only if there were an attack on the rights of the people as a whole, and therefore that only when so general a danger arises is there a right to remove or alter the legislative. But, at least in one place, this implication is rejected. 'Where the body of the people *or any single man* is deprived of their right, or is under the exercise of a power without right and have no appeal on earth, then they have a liberty to appeal to heaven whenever they judge the cause to be of sufficient moment.'[8] [My italics.]

Lest it be thought that the right to revolution so widely defined would result in continuous revolt and unrest, Locke hastens to offer reassurance. 'Nor let anyone think this lays a perpetual foundation for disorder, for this operates not until the inconvenience is so great that the majority feel it and are weary of it and find it a necessity to have it amended.'[9] This explains the final phrase in the licence to rebel quoted above 'whenever they judge the cause to be of sufficient moment'.

Locke then would seem to be saying that *ideally* rebellion is justified whenever the executive destroys the authority of the legislative or either of them act contrary to their trust. But *in fact* this will not lead to frequent revolt because of the apathy, tolerance and long-suffering patience of the people.

There are also certain corollaries to be noted. The judgement of the people is final. If they do not believe rights have been violated, or if they do not feel particularly strongly about them, there will be no rebellion. If the people, wrongly believing their rights have been violated, dismiss the legislative, there is an appeal to heaven, no doubt, but no remedy on earth. Moreover the people may use this right not to remedy wrongs but to victimise minorities; and once again the minority may have an appeal to heaven but no remedy on earth.

It may be supposed that this conclusion is a simple recognition of the force of facts, as Locke's original defence of majority decisions suggested. A body moves under the impulse of the strongest force operating in it or on it; and in a society that force is the majority. But, as we have already noticed, this is not the case. Rebellion is not a mere recognition of the power of the majority; it is the triumph of one of the three ideals on which, as we noted above (pp. 158–9) the state is founded. The ideal is that of consent or, as we should say, citizen-participation or self-determination. It is not merely that in any society the majority necessarily gets its way. As we now know from the examples of Czechoslovakia, Hungary, Rhodesia and South Africa, external or internal pressures can ensure that the majority is kept under. It is rather that citizens should share in the responsibility for their political affairs and this necessitates majority decision. Locke puts what is effectively the same point in terms of his trust doctrine.

Here, it is likely, the common question will be made: Who shall be judge whether the prince or legislature act contrary to their trust? This, perhaps, ill-affected and factious men may spread amongst the people when the prince only makes use of his due prerogative. To this I reply: the people shall be judge, for who shall be judge whether the trustee or deputy acts well and according to the trust reposed in him but he who deputes him?[16]

20 Religious Toleration

The Background. In 1685 Locke was living in Holland incognito in the house of a Dutch friend and writing the final draft of his *Essay Concerning Human Understanding*. He had completed Book II when he broke off to write his *First Letter Concerning Toleration*.

The subject of religious toleration was one of the liveliest topics of controversy both in England and on the Continent. The Civil War had raised it in an acute form, and the history of Protestant sects in the Low Countries had underlined its importance. The western world was in transition from the theocracy of the Middle Ages to the liberal secular state of the nineteenth century. Great authors both in England and abroad had contributed to the controversy. In England Hobbes' *Leviathan* was met by the arguments for toleration launched by Milton. Abroad, Bayle defending toleration faced Bossuet who urged the stamping out of 'error'. Locke was drawn into this debate by two factors.

His patron, Lord Shaftesbury, had been a strong supporter of toleration at a time when Locke held quite different views (as shown below) and it was he who brought Locke to study the topic and to swing round from his early views. Shaftesbury himself was impressed by the economic argument for toleration. Persecution of dissenters produced conflict at home and encouraged the emigration of the most independent and vigorous people among the persecuted sects. Under his influence, in 1667 and the following years, Locke wrote four drafts of a paper on Toleration. These drafts contain all the main arguments of his *First Letter*, though it was not published until over twenty years later.

Its publication was the result of the second main influence noted above. When Shaftesbury fell in 1683, Locke fled to Holland.

There he became friendly with Limborch and the Remonstrants, an Arminian sect to which his Dutch host, Veen, belonged. Limborch gave him an interest in theology and religion, and thus provided a positive basis for the negative side of toleration. Moreover, as Leclerc said, Holland was at that time buzzing with debate on this subject. So the atmosphere favoured publication of Locke's views. Even so, his *Letter* (in Latin) was published anonymously and the English version (by W. Pottle) was not admitted by Locke as his own until 1704, in a codicil to his will.

Locke's Earlier Views. Among Locke's papers have been found two documents which show his first reactions to the problem of the relations between Church and State. Both of them attack the tolerationist views of other writers. Henry Stubbe had written a history of toleration and a defence of its extension to all religions. In 1659 Locke wrote to Stubbe objecting to the proposal to extend toleration to Roman Catholics, because of their allegiance to two different authorities, one of which they believed to be both infallible and holy. This presented an inevitable threat to the security of the nation. His refusal to extend toleration to Papists remained Locke's consistent doctrine throughout his life, and the reason he gives is always the same: the threat to national security.

The second and much more important document is his work of 1660: *Two Treatises on the Civil Magistrate* (edited by P. Abrams under the title *Two Tracts on Government*: Cambridge 1967). The first treatise is entitled *Question? Whether the Civil Magistrate may lawfully impose and determine the use of indifferent things in relation to religious worship*. It is an *ad hominem* reply to a work by E. Bagshawe arguing that individuals should be free in regard to religious rites and ceremonies. Locke sticks closely to Bagshawe's text and provides no theoretical basis for his own views. This is provided by the second tract.

The historical situation does much to explain the issue. Christ Church had mirrored the divisions throughout the country on the use of vestments, the practice of kneeling or standing etc. The Restoration of 1660 was welcomed by Locke as putting an end to a period of chaos and confusion.

The argument turns on the conception of 'indifferent' matters. These are matters on which there is no prescription (for or against) by natural law or by divine law. The distinction is not an easy one, and Locke's difficulties about natural law made it no easier for him. But, for the present purpose, this does not matter, because Locke and his opponents were agreed that the details of religious rites and ceremonies were 'indifferent' in this sense, and it was about these that the conflict arose. Bagshawe argued that, since neither natural nor divine law pointed the way in these matters, they should be left to the individual conscience. He does not deny that 'order and decency' should prevail in religious observances, but he makes two powerful points. First, he urges that it is not necessary that the same order should prevail in all religions; variety and order are perfectly compatible. Secondly, order for a Christian should be voluntarily adopted, not forcibly imposed.

Locke's position is that things indifferent should be subject to the control of the magistrate, and the magistrate must be left free to decide which matters are indifferent. Even when this leads a magistrate to impose unnecessary and oppressive restrictions, the citizen is obliged to obey him. Such a magistrate 'would not perhaps be innocent and though he should not be liable to the censures of men yet would not escape the tribunal of God. However this would not discharge our obedience. And I think 'tis no no paradox to affirm that subjects may be obliged to obey those laws which it may be sinful for the magistrate to enact.'[1]

The argument for this authority is that it is required for the maintenance of peace and order. There appears to be a confusion here between 'establishing order' (in the sense of eliminating disputes and providing regularity and uniformity) and 'establishing peace' (in the sense of avoiding bloodshed, war and civil commotion). Locke attempts to show that the latter aim is involved in two ways. First, he says that if matters which are religiously indifferent are left free, then all indifferent matters will be left free; there will then be no law and no government. Secondly, he insists that private judgment in religious affairs leads to eager 'readiness for violence and cruelty' and 'grows into dangerous factions and tumults', especially 'among a people that are ready to conclude God dishonoured upon every small deviation from that way of his worship which either education or interest hath made sacred to them and that therefore they ought to vindicate the cause of God with swords in their hands and rather to fight for this honour than their own'.[2]

Nevertheless it remains clear that the desire for order in the first sense – 'order and decency', as Locke significantly describes it – was a powerful motive in his mind; and he himself recognises in his later work on Toleration that disorder in the first sense (lack of uniformity) does not necessarily lead to disorder in his second (breach of the peace); that 'wearing a cape or surplice in church can no more alarm or threaten the peace of the state than wearing a cloak or coat in the market'.

The basic difficulty in Locke's position is that the matters he calls 'indifferent' – making the sign of the cross in baptism, the surplice in preaching, kneeling at the sacrament, bowing at the name of Jesus – are not regarded as indifferent by those concerned. Conflicts of conscience are inevitable. Locke argues that obedience to law is a moral obligation; but this is circular because the issue is whether there should be laws imposing uniformity in religion. He adds that 'if private men's judgments were the moulds wherein laws were to be cast 'tis a question whether we should have any at all'.[3] This is a *non sequitur*, since the question is not whether men's consciences should determine the law but whether they should be independent of it. Locke has really no answer to Bagshawe's argument that, if the imposition of religious uniformity meets with conscientious opposition, it can succeed only by fostering hypocrisy.

The Transition to Toleration. Between 1660 when Locke wrote the *First Treatise on the Civil Magistrate* and 1667 when he drafted his *First Letter Concerning Toleration*[4], he changed his position completely. In 1667 he maintains that all speculative opinions (such as belief in the Trinity, purgatory, transubstantiation, Christ's personal reign on earth) should be tolerated because they do not concern society at all. This expressly excludes atheistical beliefs, because a belief in God is the foundation of all morality and without it man is to be counted a beast and so incapable of all society. The change from 1660 appears when Locke adds that 'divine worship' is also to be excluded from state control. He still maintains that the magistrate should control indifferent things so far as they tend to 'peace, safety and security', but purely religious observances cannot disturb the state or injure its citizens. And he now recognises that 'in worship nothing is indifferent, for all worship is concerned with what the worshipper believes acceptable to God.'

This is indeed a complete volte-face, as Cranston says.[5] J. W. Gough tends to play down the change. He points out that Locke's basic principles were substantially unchanged, though he became more liberal in the application of them.[6] This is true, but an 'application' which completely liberates the religious rites and practices of nonconforming sects was in Locke's time as important a change as could be imagined. In addition, there is a significant change in the interpretation of the principle itself. For the magistrate is now clearly limited to questions of peace and safety. Disorder – in the sense of a variety of religious practices, a 'chaos' in worship, which was what the 1660 tract set out to remedy – no longer justifies his interference.

The change in Locke's position may reflect a change in his personal situation. In 1660 he was at Christ Church, destined for the priesthood, depressed and shocked by the controversies on vestments, kneeling etc., which had divided and swung the college back and forth. In 1661 the Act of Uniformity gave him what he wanted. By 1667 he was helping his new patron, Lord Shaftesbury, to make his case to the king to establish religious toleration, a cause from which Shaftesbury had never wavered. But a rational basis for the change has also been plausibly suggested. It is that, as his MS notes show, he became increasingly interested in the accounts brought back by travellers showing the varieties of views on religion and morals prevalent among different peoples. At the same time his enquiries on natural law were making him more and more doubtful about the general capacity of human reason to attain truth in these fields. As a result no human being, not even a magistrate, could be relied on to avoid subjectivism and error, and consequently men should be left to form their own opinions on these matters.

ARGUMENTS FOR TOLERATION

In the following sections the arguments advanced by Locke for religious toleration will be arranged under four heads: (*i*) general arguments from the nature of religion; (*ii*) general arguments on the functions of churches and states; (*iii*) arguments resting on specifically Christian beliefs; and (*iv*) arguments on the contemporary issue (the penalisation of dissenters in England). Under a fifth head will be surveyed his arguments for excluding from toleration certain beliefs and practices.

(*i*) *General Arguments from the Nature of Religion*

1. No man's soul can be committed to the care of any other man. Salvation can be attained only by the will of the individual man assisted by Divine Grace. External force cannot save souls.[7]

2. 'All the life and power of true religion consist in the inward and full persuasion of the mind.'[8] 'I may be cured of some disease by remedies I have not faith in; but I cannot be saved by a religion I distrust.'[9]

3. Religion includes both speculative and practical elements. Speculative opinions cannot be imposed by law because the law cannot command what is impossible, and beliefs do not depend on a man's will or choice.[10] It might be thought that the practical side of religion, which is concerned with conduct and external rites and ceremonies, should be subject to state control. But, provided that a man's conduct and religious practices do not violate the right of any other man, they should be left alone, because he believes that they contribute to his own salvation and 'the care of each man's salvation belongs only to himself'.[11]

4. State compulsion in matters of religion can result in only outward conformity. Persecution aimed at bringing men to 'the true religion' is therefore self-defeating.[12]

5. Such persecution is effective only against those of weak will and its effect is hypocrisy.[13]

6. In any case, conscience cannot be defeated. Anyone directed by law to do what he thinks wrong should 'abstain from the actions that he judges unlawful; and he is to undergo the punishment which it is not unlawful for him to bear'.[14]

Comment. These arguments against religious persecution when the persecution is based on religious grounds are unanswerable. The only weakness in them is in the third argument where it is maintained that beliefs cannot be state-imposed. This overlooks the possibilities of 'instruction' and the techniques of brain-washing. But the arguments were valid against the opponents to whom they were addressed; for the issue was penal legislation against dissenters, and it is clear that beliefs cannot be inculcated by these means. It is also to be remembered that the effects of 'instruction' are not necessarily permanent, nor are those of brain-washing; and in both cases the shedding of the imposed belief may be accompanied by a violent reaction.

(ii) General arguments on State and Church

1. The purpose of government is the protection of civil interests and the punishment of those who violate the rights of others. This leaves to the individual liberty with respect to his own eternal salvation.[15]

2. This liberty of religion is only one particular case of the general right of every individual to be left alone in what concerns his own welfare. 'No man complains of the ill-management of his neighbour's affairs. No man is angry with another for an error committed in sowing his land or marrying his daughter. Nobody corrects a spendthrift for consuming his substance in taverns.'[16]

3. A church is a voluntary association of men joining each other of their own accord for the public worship of God. Like any other voluntary association it will require rules, to which its members must consent; but these rules must be made 'by the members themselves or by those whom the members have authorised thereunto'. The only sanction for these rules should be expulsion from the society.[17]

4. The fact that the civil magistrate belongs to a particular church gives that magistrate no rights over that or any other church, nor that church any rights which any other church lacks.[18]

5. It might be supposed that a democratic government may have rights over religion which other forms of government have not, on the ground that the laws of a democratic government rest on consent. But no man can consent to abandon the care of his own salvation to another.[19]

6. When a government attempts to dictate religious beliefs or practices, it is liable to drive the most principled and conscientious of its opponents into resistance. 'For if men enter into seditious conspiracies, it is not religion which inspires them to it in their meetings, but their sufferings and oppressions. . . . Just and moderate governments are everywhere quiet, everywhere safe.'[20]

Comment. These arguments, too, are effective and convincing, granted Locke's general views on the limitation of government action to the protection of individual rights and the exclusion from its province of 'self-regarding actions'. This limitation is discussed above (pp. 164–6).

(iii) Arguments resting on Christian beliefs

1. Christianity does not aim at external pomp or ecclesiastical dominion or compulsive force but at virtue and piety.[21]

2. Its attitude to others is one of love, not of violence.[22]

3. Its disciples are bidden to suffer, not to inflict, persecution.[23]

4. They are to show charity, meekness and toleration, as among the duties of peace and good will to all men.[24]

G*

5. Vice is a greater evil than dissent. Those who persecute in the name of religion should be asked why they do not turn their swords against 'those of their own communion that are tainted with enormous vices'. 'These are . . . more contrary to the glory of God, to the purity of the church, and to the salvation of souls than any conscientious dissent from ecclesiastical decision or separation from public worship whilst accompanied with innocency of life.'[25]

Comment. Here also Locke is on strong ground and no effective answer to him seems possible.

(iv) Arguments on the Specific Issue
As we have seen, the issue with which Locke had been concerned before was the penalisation of dissenters in England, to further uniformity in matters indifferent (that is, not prescribed by natural law or revelation).

1. In Locke's view, the matters at stake really were trifling in comparison with the basic elements of religion.

Why am I beaten and ill-used by others because, perhaps, I wear not buskins; . . . because, perhaps ,I have not been dipt in the right fashion; because I eat flesh upon the road, or some other food which agrees with my stomach, . . . or, in fine, because I follow a guide that either is, or is not, clothed in white and crowned with a mitre? . . . For the most part they are such frivolous things as these that, without any prejudice to religion or the salvation of souls, if not accompanied with superstition or hypocrisy, might either be observed or omitted; . . . which breed implacable enmities among Christian brethren who are all agreed in the substantial and truly fundamental part of religion.[26]

2. But Locke recognises that these 'frivolous things' are taken seriously and regarded by different sects as essential to their religious life. And he then argues that this belief requires that they should be left alone. 'Whatsoever is practised in the worship of God is only so far justifiable as it is believed by those that practise it to be acceptable unto him. . . . To impose such things, therefore, upon any people, contrary to their own judgement is, in effect, to command them to offend God.'[27]

(v) *Those Excluded from Toleration*

There are some beliefs and practices, including some religious beliefs and practices, which Locke thought must not be tolerated and which require suppression by the civil power.

1. Opinions contrary to the existence of human society or to those moral rules which are necessary for the preservation of human society. It is rare that such opinions are openly proclaimed, but the Roman Catholic Church says things which imply such conclusions. It teaches that faith is not to be kept with heretics, which is equivalent to giving its own followers a monopoly in promise-making. It asserts that princes who are excommunicated forfeit their kingdoms, which is equivalent to giving its own authorities the power to depose kings.[28]

2. The Roman Catholic Church also loses any claim to toleration because its members subject themselves to an authority overriding that of their own civil government.[29] Locke had used this argument consistently against the toleration of Papists from the time of his earliest reflections on politics (in his reply to Henry Stubbe in 1659), where he objected to their allegiance to an alien authority claiming infallibility. The same exclusion for the same reason is found in the other outstanding defenders of religious toleration in Locke's day, Milton and Marvell.

3. The other group whose beliefs are fatal to society and therefore not to be tolerated are the atheists. Promises, convenants and oaths, the bonds of human society, can have no hold upon an atheist. 'The taking away of God, though but even in thought, dissolves all'.[30] The point about oaths is clear, but the general dissolution of morality is not explained in this context. It is, however, part of Locke's general moral theory, as is shown above (pp. 124–8), that only a belief in God makes moral rules binding on men.

Comment. (a) The suppression of religious beliefs which run counter to the moral rules essential to the preservation of society would be generally admitted, and examples may be found in the suppression of thuggee, infanticide and ritual murder. (b) The principle behind the suppression of Roman Catholicism has also had modern echoes in the claim that communists are necessarily potential traitors, as they owe their primary allegiance to the USSR. This argument has been weakened, though not destroyed, by the divisions in the communist world. Even if allegiance is transferred from Stalin to Mao or Ho Chi Minh, treachery, defection and espionage are still to be expected. The two factors which would weaken the argument would be a spread of the Yugoslav example, to show that communism need not be identified with puppet status, and a wider recognition of the argument that suppression of a passionately held creed drives it underground, and may make it more and not less dangerous. So it might be better to follow the line normally taken in western Europe, to recognise and tolerate the existence of communist parties and organisations, and only to interfere when sedition, spying or sabotage are actually detected.

The Controversy with Proast

Locke's *First Letter Concerning Toleration* evoked a critical reply from J. Proast – *The Argument of the Letter Concerning Toleration Briefly Considered and Answered* (1690) – and opened a controversy in which Locke wrote three further *Letters*. The Second and Third Letters are extremely long and repetitive, and at the end of the Third (which occupies 400 pages in Locke's *Collected Works*) Locke notes that his design 'not to omit anything that you might think looks like an argument in yours has made mine grow beyond the size of a letter.' The Fourth Letter is brief, because unfinished.

Proast accepted Locke's argument that beliefs cannot be imposed or changed by force. He argued that penalties should be used to make dissenters reflect and consider their religious position. He also rejected extreme or cruel penalties such as loss of estate, maiming by corporal punishment, and torture in noisome prisons, and urged 'moderate penalties' to achieve the ends in question. Locke's rejoinders make the following points.

(*a*) If penalties are required to make men reflect and consider their religious position, they are much more needed against members of the Church of England than against dissenters. For dissenters have had to face the choice of allegiance; whereas, not only in most country parishes but everywhere, many members of the national church are grossly ignorant. And interest leads men into the national church to receive state protection and preferment. [31]

(*b*) Why should those dissenters who have reflected and considered be penalised? It is as if a law penalising all stammerers were defended as a penalty for swearing. [32]

(*c*) Proast would provide suitable penalties only for those who are yielding and corrigible, not those who are desperately perverse and obstinate; but how, except by punishing all, can it be known who are desperately perverse and obstinate.?[33]

(d) How much punishment is required and what should be its nature? Torture in noisome prisons is forbidden, but is imprisonment allowed? Maiming by corporal punishment is forbidden, but is corporal punishment allowed? Loss of estate is excluded, but what about loss of half or a quarter? How can the degrees be determined? – especially when the fault ('not considering') is undefined and the guilt unprovable.[34] And how long should the punishment continue? Until the wrongdoer is cured? But what is the criterion for a cure? Only conversion to the 'true relgion'? But surely a man may 'consider' and yet remain a dissenter.[35]

(e) Is there only one true religion without which a man cannot be saved? In that case a man is damned by his birthplace.[36]

(f) Who is to determine which is the true religion? Proast himself? 'Are you not persuaded that the Church of England is in the right and all that dissent from her are in the wrong ... and by that persuasion the magistrate must be directed in the use of force ... what is this but covertly to say that it is the duty of all magistrates to use force to bring men to embrace the religion of the Church of England?'[37]

(g) The only alternative to this is that the magistrate himself must judge what is the true religion. The argument in (f) would require Roman Catholic magistrates to penalise Roman Catholic citizens for not adhering to the Church of England. But if the magistrate determines what is the true religion, this would require that members of the Church of England should be penalised for belonging to that church everywhere outside England.[33] In this connection Locke urges that it is not possible for anyone to know the truth in religious matters, though this does not lead him to discard the notion of a true religion in favour of complete relativity in religious affairs. Proast meets this view – that magistrates have to act on belief in religious matters, since knowledge is unattainable – by saying that there is

a third sort of persuasion which, though not grounded upon strict demonstration, yet in firmness and stability does far exceed that which is built upon slight appearances of probability; being grounded upon such clear and solid proof as leaves no reasonable doubt in an attentive and unbiased mind: so that it approaches very near to that which is produced by demonstration, and is therefore, as it respects religion, very frequently and familiarly called in Scripture not faith or belief only, but knowledge, and in divers places full assurance. Now this kind of persuasion, this knowledge, this full assurance men may and ought to have of the true religion: but they can never have it of a false one. And this it is that must point out that religion to the magistrate which he is to promote by the method you contend for.[39]

Locke replies that degrees of firmness in persuasion would establish 'not three but three hundred sorts of persuasion . . . Men in all religions have equally strong persuasions. . . . The true religion is not always embraced with the firmest assent . . . nor is there among the many absurd religions of the world almost any one that does not find votaries to lay down their lives for it.'[40]

Comment. Locke's case against Proast, though made at inordinate length and with endless repetitions, is complete and effective. And it provides a good general case against any attempt to use penalties in order to make opportunities for people to change their views. Taken together the four *Letters* show Locke's increasing awareness that reason cannot establish religious truth and that variations in religious belief in different parts of the world form a main ground for religious toleration.

Notes

References to *Works* are to *The Works of John Locke* (London 1823) in ten volumes.

Three-number references without any title (e.g. 1 x 4) are to the *Essay Concerning Human Understanding* (6th edition).

1. SIMPLE AND COMPLEX IDEAS

1. I i 8
2. II i 2
3. II ii 2
4. II vii 10
5. II v 1
6. II xiii 2
7. II xv 9
8. Ib.
9. Ib.
10. Ib.
11. *Essay*, Draft c: R. I. Aaron, *John Locke*, p. 62
12. II xviii 4
13. III i 1
14. II ix 8
15. II xix 1
16. Ib. 2
17. II xviii 2–4
18. II xii 1
19. Ib.
20. II xxii 1
21. II xxiii 1
22. II xiii 11
23. II xvi 1
24. II xxv 5

2. PRIMARY AND SECONDARY QUALITIES

1. II viii 8–10
2. Ib. 7
3. Ib. 8
4. Ib. 10
5. Ib. 9
6. Ib. 23
7. Ib. 11
8. Ib. 12
9. Ib. 15
10. Ib. 18
11. II xxi 73
12. II viii 22

13. II xxiii 11
14. Ib. 12–14
15. II viii 16
16. Ib. 19
17. Ib. 3
18. Ib. 20
19. II xxiii 11
20. II viii 21
21. II xxxii 15
22. II viii 18
23. This connection has been demonstrated by M. Man-delbaum; *Philosophy, Science and Sense Perception*, Baltimore 1964
24. J. Bennett, 'Substance, Reality and Primary Qualities', *American Philosophical Quarterly* 1965. Reprinted in C. B. Martin and D. M. Armstrong (eds), *Locke and Berkeley*, pp. 86ff.
25. *Essay*, Draft C: Aaron *John Locke*, p. 69

3. SUBSTANCE

1. II xii 6
2. II xxiii 3
3. Stillingfleet, *Vindication of the Trinity. Works* 1720, Vol. III, p. 504
4. *Letter 1: Works,* Vol. IV, pp. 16–17
5. II xxiii 2
6. *Letter 1: Works,* Vol. IV, p. 21
7. Ib.
8. Ib.
9. I iv 18
10. *Letter III: Works,* Vol. IV, p. 447
11. *Letter 1: Works,* Vol. IV, p. 33
12. II xxiii 2
13. Leibniz, *New Essays,* II xxiii 2
14. II xiii 18
15. *Letter 1: Works,* Vol. IV, p. 33
16. II xxiii 1
17. Ib. 6
18. Aaron, *John Locke,* p. 69
19. *New Essays,* II xxiii 2
20. Leibniz, *New Essays,* II xii 6
21. Ib. II xxiii

4. POWER

1. II xxi 1, 6
2. Ib. 1
3. Ib. 3
4. Ib. 2
5. Aaron, *John Locke,* p. 69
6. II vii 8
7. II xxi 4
8. IV iii 29
9. II xxi 11
10. II xxi 1
11. II xxvi 1
12. Hume, *Treatise of Human Nature,* Book I, Pt. III, Sec. ii: Selby-Bigge (ed.), p. 78
13. Ib. Sec. iii, p. 82
14. II xxi 4
15. IV x 3
16. *Letter 1: Works,* Vol. IV, pp. 61–2
17. II xxi 2

18. Ib. 5. Cf. ɪɪ vii 3
19. Cf. the case of Mr Hanna, in Sidis and Goodhart, *Multiple Personality*, pp. 91–2, 107–8, 203–4

5. ABSTRACT GENERAL IDEAS

1. ɪɪ xi 9
2. ɪ ii 15
3. ɪɪ xii 3
4. ɪɪ xi 9
5. *Essay*, Draft c: Aaron, *John Locke*, p. 65
6. Berkeley, *Principles of Human Knowledge*, Intro., § xii
7. Hume, *Enquiry concerning Human Understanding*, xii, Pt. ii: Selby-Bigge (ed.), § 124N, p. 158
8. Aaron, *John Locke*, p. 197
9. ɪɪ xi 9
10. ɪɪɪ iii 6
11. Berkeley; *Principles*, Intro., § xvi
12. ɪɪ xviii 4
13. ɪɪɪ iii 7
14. Ib. 8
15. Ib. 9
16. *Remarks on some of Mr Norris's Books*, para. 4: *Works*, Vol. x, p. 250
17. ɪɪɪ iii 11
18. Ib. 13
19. Stillingfleet, *Vindication of the Trinity. Works*, 1710, Vol. ɪɪɪ, p. 511
20. *Letter ɪ Works*, Vol. ɪv, p. 86
21. Ib. p. 87 (quoting ɪɪɪ vi 28)
22. Ib.
23. Stillingfleet, *Vindication*, p. 511
24. *Letter ɪ:* p. 90 (Cf. ɪɪɪ ii 3, ɪɪɪ vi 26)
25. ɪɪɪ vi 29
26. ɪɪɪ iii 14, 17 (Cf. ɪv iv 14–16)
27. ɪɪɪ vi 12
28. ɪɪɪ vi 30
29. ɪɪɪ vi 40
30. ɪɪ xxii 1
31. Ib. 2

6. KNOWLEDGE OF MINDS

1. ɪɪ xix 1
2. Ib. 2
3. Ib. 1
4. *Letter ɪɪ* to Stillingfleet: *Works*, Vol. ɪv, p. 143
5. ɪɪɪ i 15
6. Ib. 16
7. Descartes, *Meditation ɪ: Discourse on Method* etc., Everyman Edition, p. 89
8. Id., *Meditation vɪ:* p. 133
9. Id., *Meditation ɪɪ:* p. 88
10. ɪɪ ix 1
11. ɪɪ i 8
12. ɪɪ vii 1 (Cf. ɪɪ xx 1)
13. ɪɪ xx 2
14. ɪɪ xxi 12
15. ɪɪɪ i 19
16. ɪɪ xxvii 9
17. Ib. 10

18. II i 7
19. IV xxi 4

20. II xxiii 36
21. IV xi 12

7. Personal Identity; and Mind-and-Body

1. II xxvii 3
2. Ib. 4
3. Ib.
4. Ib. 5
5. Ib. 6
6. Ib. 10
7. Ib. 13
8. Ib. 20
9. Morton Prince, *The Dissociation of a Personality*, p. 144
10. A. G. N. Flew, in *Philosophy*, 1951; reprinted Martin and Armstrong (eds), *Locke and Berkeley*, p. 155
11. H. P. Grice, in *Mind*, 1941
12. D. Wiggins, *Identity and Spatio-Temporal Continuity*, 1967
13. II xxvii 25
14. II xxiii 19
15. IV iii 6
16. Stillingfleet, *Answer to Mr Locke's Letter: Works*, 1710, Vol. III, p. 535
17. *Letter 11: Works*, Vol. IV, pp. 457–83

8. The Freedom of the Will

1. II xxi 6
2. Ib. 14
3. Ib. 8
4. Ib. 11
5. Ib. 12
6. Ib. 24
7. Ib. 25
8. Ib. 29
9. Ib.
10. Ib. 31
11. Ib. 40
12. Ib. 47
13. Ib.
14. Ib. 48
15. Ib. 49
16. Ib. 51
17. Ib. 52
18. Ib.
19. Ib. 53
20. Ib. 56

9. Ideas

1. I i 8
2. *Examination of P. Malebranche's Opinion*, § 47: *Works*, Vol. IX, p. 287
3. Ib.
4. *Remarks upon some of Mr Norris's Books*, § 17: *Works*, Vol. X, p. 256
5. *Examination* etc., § 18: *Works*, Vol. IX, p. 220
6. Ib. pp. 234–5
7. G. A. Paul, in *Proceedings of the Aristotelian Society*, Suppl. Vol. XV, 1936
8. Cf. especially J. L. Austin, *Sense and Sensibilia*, 1962

9. G. Ryle, *The Concept of Mind*, ch. VIII
piricist Theory of Memory',
10. R. F. Holland, 'The Em-
Mind, 1954
11. A. D. Woozley, *The Theory of Knowledge*, pp. 64-5
12. II xxx iii
13. Ib. 20
14. *Works*, Vol. IV, p. 60
15. H. W. B. Joseph, in *Mind*, 1927

16. G. Ryle, in *Proceedings of the Aristotelian Society*, 1929-30
17. Descartes, *Remarks on the Programme of Regius: Works*, Haldane and Ross (eds), Vol. I, p. 442
18. J. W. Yolton, *Locke and the Way of Ideas*, ch. II
19. I ii 2-4
20. I ii 14
21. I ii 7-12
22. I ii 18
23. Cf. Yolton, op. cit.

10. KNOWLEDGE

1. IV i 2
2. Ib. 3
3. IV xii 14-5
4. IV iv 6
5. Ib. 8
6. IV xii 15 (Cf. IV vii 10)
7. II xx 2-3
8. II xiii 2
9. Ib. 4
10. Ib. 4-6
11. IV iv 6
12. *Third Letter: Works*, Vol. IV, pp. 404-5
13. IV vii
14. *Essays on the Law of Nature*, W. von Leyden (ed.), p. 145
15. I ii 16
16. IV iii 9
17. Ib. 10
18. Ib. 14
19. Ib. 15
20. Ib. 16
21. II xxxiii 1
22. Ib. 5

23. *Conduct of the Understanding*, § 41: *Works*, Vol. III, p. 276
24. Ib. p. 277
25. IV iii 9
26. IV iv 3
27. *Examination of P. Malebranche's Opinion*, § 51: *Works*, Vol. IX, p. 250
28. Quoted by Locke, *Third Letter: Works*, Vol. IV, p. 297
29. *Third Letter*, p. 360
30. IV ix 2
31. Ib. 3
32. IV ii 14
33. IV xi 5
34. Ib. 8 (Cf. Ib. 14)
35. Ib. 3
36. *First Letter to Stillingfleet: Works*, Vol. IV, p. 77
37. *Of Education*, § 193 *Works*, Vol. IX, p. 185
38. IV iii 16
39. Ib. 26
40. IV vi 13

41. IV ii 11–13
42. *Examination* etc., § 9: *Works*, Vol. IX, pp. 215–6
43. Ib. § 70, p. 217. (Cf. *Remarks upon some of Mr Norris's Books*, § 15: *Works*, Vol. X, pp. 254–5.)
44. IV iii 26

45. Ib. 25
46. IV vi 11
47. IV xii 9
48. Ib. 13
49. IV xvi 4
50. IV xiv 2
51. IV xii 11

11. LANGUAGE AS A SOURCE OF ERROR

1. III v 15
2. III ix 9
3. III x 33
4. III ix 9
5. II xiii 19
6. III x 6 (Cf. II xiii 1)
7. III x 33
8. III ix 6
9. Ib. 13 (Cf. Ib. 17)

10. II xxi 6
11. III x 14
12. Ib. 15
13. II xiii 28
14. III ix 7–9
15. III x 22
16. II xxi 20
17. Ib.

12. MORAL PRINCIPLES

1. *Epistle to the Reader: Works*, Vol. I, p. *xlvi*
2. W. von Leyden, *John Locke: Essays on the Law of Nature*, 1954; 'John Locke and Natural Law', *Philosophy*, 1956
3. *Two Tracts on Government*, P. Abrams (ed.) 1967, to which notes 4–6 in section II (*i*) of this chapter refer.
4. pp. 124–5
5. pp. 222–3
6. p. 226
7. *Essays on the Law of Nature*, W. von Leyden (ed.) 1954, to which notes 8–33 in section II (*ii*) of this chapter refer.

8. p. 109
9. 183
10. pp. 185–7
11. p. 189
12. p. 111
13. p. 113
14. Ib.
15. p. 183
16. p. 199
17. pp. 183–5
18. p. 145
19. p. 131
20. p. 149
21. p. 111
22. p. 125
23. p. 131
24. pp. 133, 151–5
25. p. 157

26. pp. 109, 155, 183

27. pp. 111, 149

28. p. 111

29. pp. 113, 115

30. pp. 205–7

31. p. 195

32. p. 129

33. p. 203

34. Draft A: Aaron and Gibb (eds), §26

35. For text, see von Leyden, *Essays, etc.*, pp. 265ff.

36. II xx.

37. Von Leyden, p. 265

38. Ib. p. 267

39. Ib.

40. Ib. p. 269

41. First published by W. von Leyden in *Philosophy*, 1956, p. 23

42. Ib. p. 35

43. Printed in Lord King's *Life*, 1858, pp. 308–13

44. *Essays on the Law of Nature*, p. 70

45. *Of Ethick in General*, §8

46. Aaron, *John Locke* p. 260

47. *Essays on the Law of Nature*, p. 71, NI

48. M. Cranston, *John Locke*, p. 123 (MS. Locke, c. 28 ff. 143–4)

49. Not in King's *Life*; first published by von Leyden, *Essays* etc., p. 70

50. Aaron and Gibb, §26

51. Von Leyden, *Essays* etc., p. 70

52. I iii 4

53. I iii 1

54. IV iv 7 (Cf. IV xi 8)

55. III xi 15

56. Ib. 16

57. IV iv 8

58. III xi 16

59. IV iii 18

60. IV iv 8

61. Ib. 9

62. III xi 15 17

63. IV iii 19

64. Von Leyden, *Essays* etc., pp. 9, 13

65. Ib. pp. 85–8

66. Appended to the *Second Letter* to Stillingfleet: *Works*, Vol. IV, pp. 186–9

67. *Works*, Vol. IX p. 291

68. Ib. p. 294

69. Ib. p. 377

70. III ix 23

71. *Works*, Vol. VII, p. 139

72. Ib. p. 140

73. Ib. p. 141

74. Ib. p. 143

75. I iii 12

76. IV xi 13

77. Quoted Aaron, *John Locke* p. 263

78. II xxviii 8

79. IV xiii 4

80. IV xi 8 (Cf. II vii 3, IV xi 3)

81. II xx 2. (Cf. II xxi 42)

82. II xx 3

83. II xxi 33

84. II xx 6

85. II xxi 29

86. II xxi 40 (Cf. 30, 31, 35, 41)

87. Ib. 47

88. Ib. 43

89. Ib. 55–70

90. Ib. 43

91. Ib. 44

92. Ib. 45
93. Ib.
94. Ib. 63
95. 1 iii 5
96. Ib. 6
97. Ib.
98. 1 iii 12
99. Ib. 13
100. 11 xxviii 5
101. Ib. 8
102. 1 iii 8
103. 11 xxi 35
104. Ib. 55–70

105. 11 xxi 55
106. Bentham, *Introduction to the Principles of Morals and Legislation*, iii. 1: Selby-Bigge (ed.), *British Moralists* Vol. 1, § 378
107. Butler, *Sermon XI*: Selby-Bigge (ed.), *British Moralists*, Vol. 1, § 239
108. *Works*, Vol. VII, p. 139
109. Ib. p. 149
110. Ib. p. 150

13. THEOLOGY AND RELIGION

1. 1 iv 2–8
2. Ib. 13
3. Ib. 15
4. IV iii 18
5. 11 xxiii 33
6. IV x 7
7. IV x 2–12
8. 11 xvii 13
9. IV x 10
10. 1 iv 9
11. Stillingfleet, *Works*, 1720, Vol. III, p. 508
12. *First Letter: Works*, Vol. IV, pp. 47–9
13. IV xix 17
14. Ib. 5
15. Ib. 14
16. IV xvi 14
17. *Second Letter* to Stillingfleet: *Works*, Vol. IV, p. 341
18. IV xix 4
19. IV xviii 4
20. Ib. 5

21. Ib. 9
22. *Epistola de Tolerantia*, R. Klibansky (ed.), tr. Gough, p. 26
23. *Works*, Vol. III, pp. 20–31
24. Ib. p. 101
25. *Vindication of the Reasonableness of Christianity. Works*, Vol. VII, p. 178
26. Ib. p. 157
27. Ib. pp. 151–8
28. Ib. p. 102
29. Ib. p. 105
30. Ib. p. 139
31. Stillingfleet, *Works*, 1720, Vol. III, p. 509
32. *First Letter: Works*, Vol. IV, pp. 66–8
33. Stillingfleet, *Works*, 1720, Vol. III pp. 564, 8
34. *Second Vindication: Works*, Vol. VII, p. 350
35. Ib. p. 387

14. THE TWO TREATISES

1. P. Laslett (ed.), *John Locke: Two Treatises of Government,* 1960

15. THE STATE OF NATURE

1. *Second Treatise: Two Treatises of Government,* P. Laslett (ed.) 1960, § 4
2. Ib.
3. § 54
4. *Conduct of the Understanding.* § 2: *Works,* Vol. III, p. 207
5. *Second Treatise,* § 4
6. § 6
7. § 19
8. §123
9. §136
10. §8
11. §124
12. §7
13. §11
14. §13
15. §19
16. Laslett (ed.), *Two Treatises,* Introduction p. 98
17. Hobbes, *Leviathan,* Pt. I, ch. 13, Everyman Edition, p. 64
18. *Second Treatise,* §123
19. §127
20. *Works,* Vol. VI, p. 42

16. PROPERTY

1. *Second Treatise: Two Treatises,* Laslett (ed.), § 26, 28
2. §§39, 40, 43
3. §§ 31, 46
4. §§36, 37, 46, 50
5. §46
6. §116 (Cf. §72)
7. Ib.
8. §183
9. §28
10. §43
11. §85
12. §41
13. §37
14. §3
15. §123 (Cf. §§71, 87)
16. *Works,* Vol. VI, pp. 9–10

17. THE FOUNDATION OF GOVERNMENT

1. *Second Treatise: Two Treatises,* Laslett (ed.), § 99
2. §138
3. §102
4. §49
5. §211
6. §77
7. §21
8. §87
9. §89
10. §212
11. §205
12. §219
13. §227
14. §§95–7 (Cf. §§98, 89)
15. §89
16. §128
17. *First Treatise,* §§144–5; *Second Treatise,* §§105, 108
18. *Second Treatise,* §102

18. The Justification of Government

1. *Second Treatise: Two Treatises*, Laslett (ed.), §93
2. §96
3. Rousseau, *Contrat Social*, IV ii
4. Ib. II iii
5. Ib. IV ii
6. Ib.
7. *Second Treatise*, §132
8. §89
9. §94
10. §134
11. §94 (Cf. §105)
12. §95
13. §117
14. §73
15. §117
16. §121
17. §85
18. §122
19. §119
20. §52
21. §§65, 66, 67, 74, etc.
22. §131
23. §135
24. §137
25. §158
26. §161
27. *First Letter: Works*, Vol. IV, p. 22
28. *Second Treatise*, §57

19. The Right of Revolution

1. *Second Treatise: Two Treatises*, Laslett (ed.) §19
2. §20
3. Laslett, *Two Treatises*, p. 299N
4. §168
5. §§212–19
6. §220
7. §221
8. §168
9. Ib. (Cf. §§223–30)
10. §240

20. Religious Toleration

1. P. Abrams (ed.), *Two Tracts on Government*, p. 152
2. Ib., pp. 121, 150, 151
3. Ib., p. 137
4. MS. Locke, c. 28 ff. 21–32
5. M. Cranston, *John Locke*, p. 67
6. J. W. Gough (ed.), *Epistola de Tolerantia*, Intro., p. 12
7. *Letters on Toleration: Works*, Vol. VI, p. 10. The remaining references in this chapter are to this source.
8. p. 10
9. p. 28
10. pp. 39–40
11. p. 41
12. pp. 318, 336, 542
13. p. 379
14. p. 43
15. pp. 9–10, 42–3, 503
16. p. 22
17. pp. 13–16
18. p. 18
19. p. 10
20. p. 49

21. p. 6
22. p. 15
23. Ib.
24. p. 21
25. p. 7
26. p. 24
27. pp. 29–30
28. p. 45
29. p. 46
30. p. 47

31. pp. 94, 340
32. p. 75
33. p. 273
34. pp. 263, 267
35. pp. 244, 293
36. p. 12
37. pp. 557, 565–6
38. pp. 366–7
39. Quoted by Locke, pp. 557–8
40. p. 563

Bibliographical Note

Bibliographies of Locke are available in R. I. Aaron, *John Locke*, pp. 312–20; and J. W. Yolton, *John Locke and the Way of Ideas*, pp. 209–32.

More comprehensive lists are given in H. O. Christopherson, *A Bibliographical Introduction to the Study of John Locke*, Oslo 1930, and (for publications since that date) R. Hall and R. Woodhouse, 'Forty Years of Work on John Locke 1929–1969', *Philosophical Quarterly*, July 1970.

The following list (included here by way of gratitude and acknowledgement, rather than guidance to scholars) notes the works which I have found of most use in writing this study.

AARON, R. I., *John Locke*, Oxford 1937; rev. edn 1954

ABRAMS, P., *John Locke: Two Tracts on Government*, Cambridge 1967

CRANSTON, M., *John Locke: A Biography*, London 1957

GOUGH, J. W., *John Locke's Political Philosophy*, Oxford 1950; rev. edn 1956

KLIBANSKY, R. and GOUGH, J. W., *John Locke: Epistola de Tolerantia*, Oxford 1968

LASLETT, P., *John Locke: Two Treatises of Government*, Cambridge 1960; rev. imp. 1963

LEYDEN, W. VON, *John Locke: Essays on the Law of Nature*, Oxford 1954

MACPHERSON, C. B., *The Political Theory of Possessive Individualism: Hobbes to Locke*, Oxford 1962

YOLTON, J. W., *John Locke and the Way of Ideas*, London 1956

There is an edition of Locke's *Essay Concerning Human Understanding* by J. W. YOLTON in the Everyman series (Dent, London; Dutton, New York), and an abridged edition in Fontana Books by A. D. WOOZLEY.

Index

197